BEGINNER'S GUIDE TO PLAYING THE PIANO PROFESSIONALLY

Tips & Guide to Enhance Your Piano Playing Skill

LEVEL 2

ELVINE ROBERT

Copyright © 2018 Elvine Robert

All rights reserved. No segment of this book or any portion therein may be distributed, reproduced or transmitted in whatsoever manner, including photocopying, recording or any other means of transmission without the express written permission of the writer, except for brief citations in a book review.

DEDICATION

This book is dedicated to every and anyone who is passionately in love with music and just want to take this passion to a greater level.

Contents

INTRODUCTION .... *

A Quick Review on Level 1 .... *

Chapter One 1

   SIGHT READING 1

   The Staff & Clef, Notes and Pitches 2

   Time Signature 14

   Tempo 17

   Key Signature 18

   Chords in sheet music 21

   Chapter Summary 22

Chapter Two 23

   MAJOR, MINOR AND DOMINANT SEVENTH CHORDS 23

   The Major Seventh Chord 24

   The dominant seventh chords 25

   The Minor Seventh Chords 28

   Inversions 29

Chapter Summary 31

Chapter Three 33

MAJOR, MINOR AND DOMINANT SEVENTH CHORD
PROGRESSIONS 33

The I-IV-I-V-I (1-4-1-5-1) Chord Progression 34

I-IV-V-IV-I Chord Progression 36

The II-V-I Chord Progression 37

The VI-II-V-I Chord Progression 40

The III-VI-II-V-I Chord Progression 42

12-Bar Blues Chord Progression 45

Chapter Summary 48

Chapter Four 49

DIMINISHED SEVENTH, MAJOR SIXTH AND MINOR
SIXTHS CHORDS 49

The Diminished Seventh Chords 49

The Half Diminished Seventh Chords 52

Major and Minor Sixth Chords 54

Chapter Summary 58

Chapter Five 59

MAJOR SIXTH, MINOR SIXTH AND DIMINISHED CHORD PROGRESSIONS 59

The Diminished Chord in the 2-5-1 Chord Progression .. 60

The Diminished Seventh Chord as Passing Chord 62

The VII-III-VI-II-V-I Chord Progression 64

Diminished Seventh chords in Gospel Progression 64

Chapter Summary 67

Chapter Six 69

MAJOR, MINOR, AND DOMINANT NINTH CHORDS 69

The Major Ninth Chords 70

Minor Ninth Chords 72

Dominant Ninth Chords 74

Dominant Ninth Chords with an Added Sixth Note 76

Learning to Play the Min9 and Dom9/6 Chord 77

The Min9 and Dom9/6 Chords to Resolve to the IV9 81

The III-VI-II-V-I to Resolve to the IV Chord 84

Using the Ninth Chords to Replace the Seventh Chords 85

The I-IV Turn-around with Ninth Chords 86

Chapter Summary 88

Chapter Seven..89

THE ELVENTH AND THIRTEENTH CHORDS 89

Major Eleventh and Thirteenth Chords 89

Minor Eleventh and Thirteenth Chords............................91

Dominant Eleventh and Thirteenth Chords......................93

Broken Chords 95

Chapter Summary 97

ABOUT THE AUTHOR

Elvine Robert is a passionate music lover who has committed himself to giving assistance to music lovers worldwide. This he does on social media platforms, with his books, etc.

Although Elvine started as a singer in a church choir, he went on to becoming a pianist and a music producer, which lead him to being of great value to his choir and others around him

INTRODUCTION

Hi there! Are you tired of being stuck and want to take that next step to playing the piano professionally? Then, you're in the right place. This book is a **beginner's guide to playing the piano level 2.**

In this book, we'll be looking at the seventh, ninth, eleventh and thirteenth chords. what we will not be looking at are triads as I have already covered this in the level one of this book.

If you don't know what triads (or three toned chords) are or how they are formed, then you should take a look at the level one of this book.

We'll not only be looking at how the above chords are formed (i.e. the seventh, ninth, eleventh and thirteenth chords), but also, how they are used and altered in chord progressions, how they are inverted to transit smoothly to the next chord in a chord progression, and how these chords are related with one another, plus lots more!

A Quick Review on Level 1

Before I take you to the next level in playing the piano professionally, I would like to take you through what we have learnt so far in the **level 1** of this book and how they all relate with one another. This would help you to have a clearer understanding of where you are coming from and where you are headed.

Let's take a look!

For clarity, I will be taking you through the **Level 1** of this book chapter by chapter.

Chapter One

This chapter was a general introduction to the piano. Here, we saw that the piano has a total number of 12 keys; with 5 of these keys being black and the remaining 7, white, and how these keys are represented with the English alphabet system. The main focus of this chapter was on piano scales; specifically, major scales, fingering techniques for playing these major scales in all 12 keys and finally, how to use the circle of fifth chart to learn the 12 major scales more easily.

At the end of this chapter, one should be able to play the 12 major scales on the piano with the right fingering technique.

Chapter Two

Now that you have learnt how to play piano scales in all 12 keys, guess what the next step is…yes, chords! This chapter was all about chords and to help you understand how chords are formed, I had to take you through what an interval is, the relationship between the different classification of intervals, how to form chords (major chords) with these intervals and finally, the inversions of these major chords. Only major chords were learnt in the 12 major keys in this chapter.

Chapter Three

Since chapter two was all about major chords and nothing more, in this chapter, I had to take you through how to make use of these major chords to form major chord progressions, where these chord progressions can be seen in songs and finally, the alteration of chords in these major chord progressions.

Chapter Four

Everything we've known so far all ended with major chords and since these major chords are inadequate to play lots of songs correctly, I had to introduce you to the concept of minor and diminished chords. The idea was to start from the different modes of a scale and from all the different mode, laid more emphasis on the Aeolian mode (also known as a natural minor scale) and from this minor scale, minor chords were formed on the 1st, 4th and 5th just like the major scale. Since a major key and its relative minor key shares the same scale, and the chords formed in both the major and relative minor scale are on the 1st, 4th and 5th note of that scale, you would notice that six (6) chords has been formed out of the 7 notes in a scale. The last note left forms a diminished chord.

Chapter Five

Now that we've learnt minor and diminished chords, plus our previous knowledge of major chords from chapter two, we had to look at different chord progressions using the major, minor and diminished chords.

In the level one of this book, learning was limited to triads (three note chords). Now, I'll be taking you a step further in playing the piano professionally. **In this book, we'll be looking at the seventh, ninth, eleventh and the thirteenth chords.**

Chapter One

SIGHT READING

Before we can go a step further into playing the piano, I thought it helpful and relevant to give you a quick insight on sheet music or sight reading. Since sheet music wasn't so much fun for me, I will do the best I possibly can to make sure it's as fun as it can possibly be for you.

If you're already familiar with the concept of sheet music, please skip this chapter.

Sheet Music; What Comes to Mind?

For someone who plays the piano but has no idea on sight reading or sheet music, sheet music to him can be related with an English man seeing a Greek written book for the first time and attempting to understand it. Sheet music is about being able to translate musical notes on paper to the real notes on the piano or any other musical instrument.

Is Sight Reading Important?

Not being able to sight read doesn't mean that you won't be able to play the piano in a way that would amaze listeners, but this also doesn't mean that you shouldn't learn it either; what have you to lose?

One of the ways I find sight reading important is that you get to play songs that you've never heard of the exact way it was played. Also, have you ever tried to learn something new on the internet; about playing your favourite instrument and all you're faced with are tons and tons of sheet music? Really frustrating, isn't it? Learning to sight read makes the whole learning process complete when learning to play the piano.

How Can I Learn to Sight Read?

In order to be able to sight read, there are keywords you should know and understand. These are the **Staff, Notes, Pitches, Clef, etc**. We'll be looking at these keywords and what they really represent in sheet music.

The Staff & Clef, Notes and Pitches

To be able to sight read, you must first get acquainted with the fundamental components of sheet music; which are the staff, the clefs, the notes and the pitches of these notes. We'll be looking at each of these components one after the other:

The staff

The staff is basically made up of five (5) horizontal lines at equal interval or space from each other and these spaces when counted is seen to be equal to four (4). We could therefore say that a staff is made up of five (5) lines and four (4) spaces.

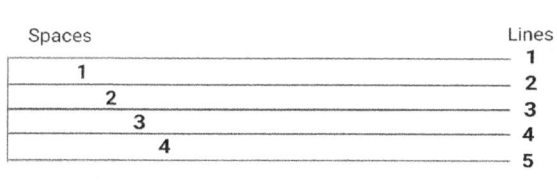

Showing a Staff with 5 Lines and 4 Spaces

Clefs

There are two types of clefs of which you should get acquainted with; these are:

1. The treble clef.
2. The bass clef.

Beginner's Guide to Playing the Piano Professionally

1. **Treble Clef**

The treble clef, also known as the **G clef** has evolved from the alphabet letter "G" to something more different but similar. A staff with the treble clef symbol (let's call it a treble clef staff) is where notes of higher pitches on the keyboard are placed.

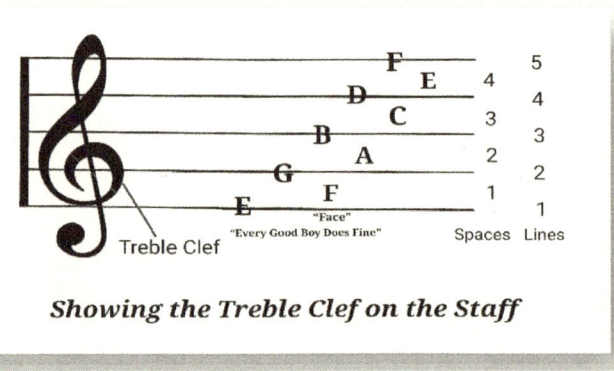

Showing the Treble Clef on the Staff

To be able to remember what note should be on the line of a treble clef staff, we remember the letters **E G B D F** by the word cue **"Every Boy Does Fine"** and for the notes in the spaces between the lines of the staff, we remember the letters **F A C E** by simply remembering the word **"FACE"**

2. **Bass Clef**

The bass clef is also known as the **F clef.** The line between the two dots of the bass clef is the **F line** (also take note of the G line on the treble clef). A staff with the bass clef symbol (let's call it a bass clef staff) is where notes of lower pitches are placed.

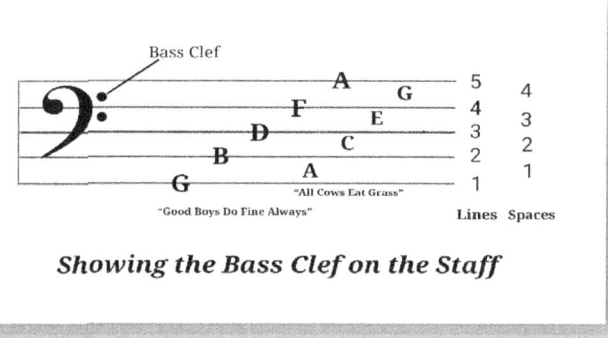

Showing the Bass Clef on the Staff

This means that lower notes on the keyboard are placed on the Bass clef staff. A very common mnemonic to remember notes on the lines and in the spaces between these lines of a bass clef staff is by remembering the letters **G B D F A** with the word cue **"Good Boys Does Fine Always"** for lines and **A C E G** with the word cue **"All Cows Eat Grass"** for spaces.

Grand Staff

A grand staff or great stave is a combination of a treble clef staff (or stave) and a bass clef staff (or stave). These two staffs are joined together with the help of a **BRACE**. When it comes to sight reading, notes on the treble clef staff are played using the right hand while notes on the Bass clef are played using the left hand.

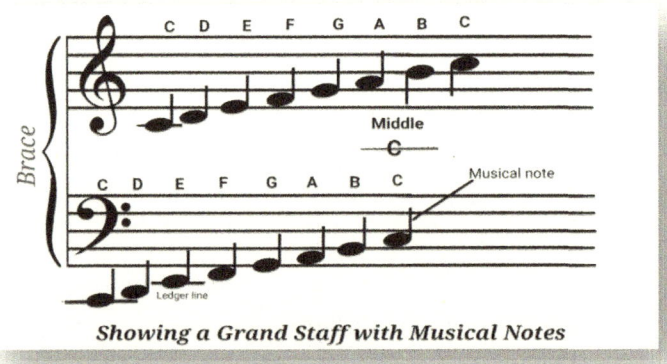

Showing a Grand Staff with Musical Notes

This means that notes on a grand staff would be for both the left and right hand depending on the position of the note on the grand staff (either it is on the treble clef staff or on the bass clef staff).

Ledger Line

Since the piano as you probably know by now; is made up of 88 notes, it wouldn't be "weird" if these notes don't fit into the grand staff. This is where the use of ledger lines come in. A ledger line is a short horizontal line which is placed above a musical staff or below it to accommodate notes which are higher or lower than the range on the staff (as shown in the above illustration).

Notes and Pitches

Notes and pitches work hand in hand, they are inseparable! For every note placed on the staff, exist a unique pitch assigned to it. A pitch can therefore be seen as the frequency of a note on a staff when played on the piano. This frequency can either be low or high depending on the position of the note played on the piano.

Notes are oval-shaped symbols that are with or without a stem and flag; which are placed on the lines or in the spaces of the staff.

Note Description

When you look at every note type, you'll discover that each of these notes has a head (which is oval-shaped) that is either filled (black) or empty (white), but you would also notice that some of these notes have a vertical extension from this head (called a stem) which extends either upward (from the right point of the note head) or downward (from the left point of the note head). The direction of this extension doesn't change how

Beginner's Guide to Playing the Piano Professionally

a note is played, but rather, serves as a way to make notes easily readable while being neatly placed on the staff. Finally, there is a note type which took it a step further by having one or more extra extension (called a flag) from this vertical extension.

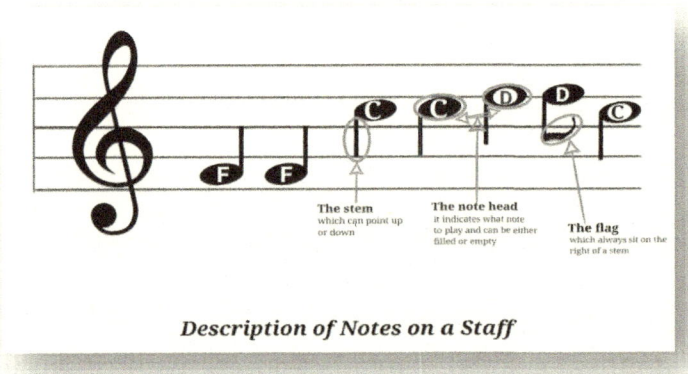

Description of Notes on a Staff

Let's imagine three college students; the first thinks he's serious with his studies but spends most of his time doing "any other thing", the second is actually serious and does all that is required of a student, while the third student isn't only serious, but takes it as his job.

Now, the first college student is like the note with just a head that is oval in shape, the second is a note with a head and a vertical extension and the third is a note with a head, a vertical extension and one or more extra extension from the vertical extension.

A note is therefore made up of three parts; the **note head**, the **stem** and the **flag.** The **position** of the **note head** on the staff will always determine what note to play on the piano or any other instrument.

Note Value

By now, it should be clear that a note is made up of three parts as I earlier mentioned. What may not be clear is how each of these parts can affect the **value** of a **note** in sheet music.

A note value has to do with how **long** a note is **held**. We'll be looking at the each of these note part and how they influence "how long" a note is held on the piano. We'll also be looking at a few other symbols which are used in sheet music to change the duration of a note.

Basically, a **note head** when without a **stem** and **flag** is called a **whole note**. This whole note is always seen to be empty (white) and is held for **four beats**.

Beginner's Guide to Playing the Piano Professionally

When a note head has a stem, it reduces the note value and the note is held for a shorter time when compared with a whole note. This note is called a **half note** and it's held for **two beats**.

Now, when the note head of this half note (which is held for two beats) is filled (i.e. black), it reduces its note value. The new note is referred to as a quarter note and it is held for **one beat**. So, for four beats, you get to play this quarter note four times on the piano.

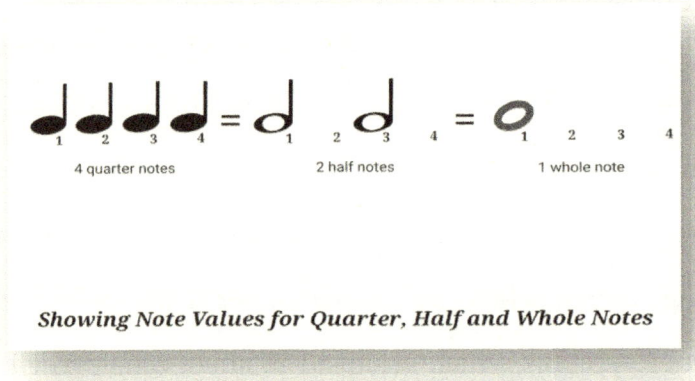

Showing Note Values for Quarter, Half and Whole Notes

The note **flag** is a curvy line which always extends from the right of the note stem. Its sole purpose is to reduce a note value (or how long a note is held) by half that note value. Note values goes from the whole note, half note, and then the quarter note before the introduction of a flag to reduce this quarter note further. Therefore, adding a **single flag** to a quarter note would result to **1/2 of a quarter note** (called an eight), a **double flag** would result to **1/4 of a quarter note** (called a sixteenth) etc.

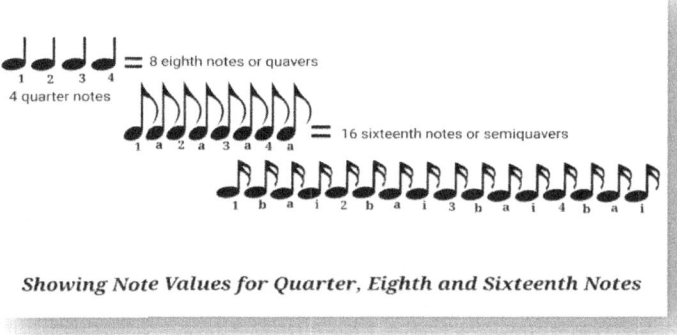

Showing Note Values for Quarter, Eighth and Sixteenth Notes

Beams do the same thing as the flags do only that it helps us to read music more clearly by arranging notes neatly on a staff. Let's see beams as two quarter note with a flag, but instead of each quarter note to have it separate flag, we make use of a straight line to combine the two quarter notes.

Beginner's Guide to Playing the Piano Professionally

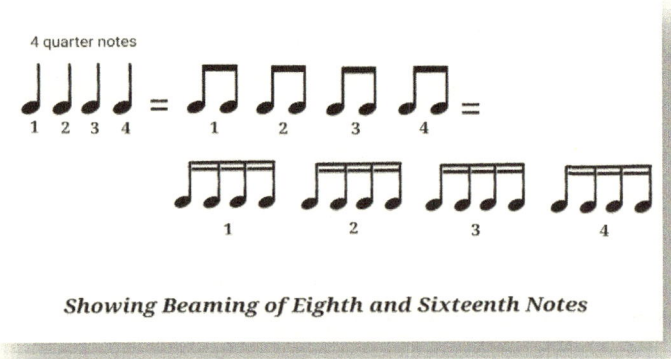

Showing Beaming of Eighth and Sixteenth Notes

Now that we're done with what shortens how long a note is held, we'll be looking at what can increase how long a note is held. This will bring us to the **Dots** and **Ties**.

Dots are used in increasing the value of a note. This is achieved by putting a dot in front of the head of a note. This increases the note value of such a note by half its original note value. For example, putting a dot in front of a half (1/2) note would increase its note value by a quarter (1/4) note. The resulting note value would then be an addition of a half note and a quarter note.

Ties can also be used to increase the amount of time a note is held. In music theory, a tie is seen as a small curved line which connects two notes of the same pitch. You can only play

Elvine Robert

these notes once, but the note value would then be the addition of the note values of both notes.

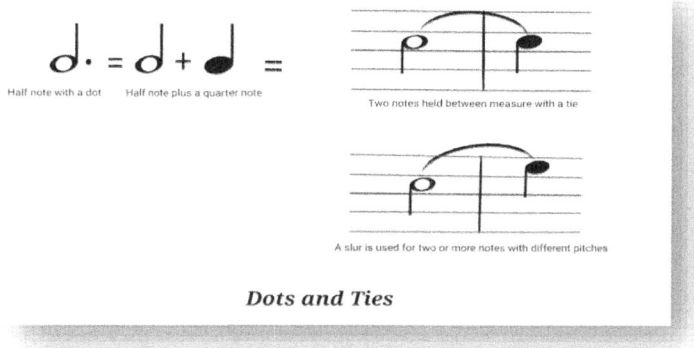

Dots and Ties

Can two notes of different pitches be connected with a tie?

The answer is no! when you see a similar curved line (sometimes the curve could cover a measure, two measure or more) used to connect two notes of different pitches, it is referred to as a slur. A slur tells you to play two notes smoothly.

Why do we make use of a tie?

A tie becomes important when a note is to be held across a bar line, it is also important when a note length is difficult to express with just one note value.

A Rest

What if there isn't a note taking each beat in a musical piece or maybe we just want a long (or short) pulse in the middle of a song, what then do we do? It's simple, we just take a rest!

A rest tells us how long a note should be held based on its shape, but only that the note being held produces no sound.

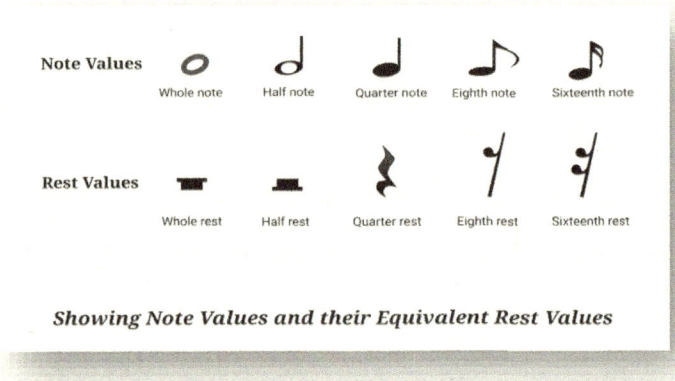

Showing Note Values and their Equivalent Rest Values

Every rest value has it equivalent note value as shown in the above image.

Time Signature

When you critically look at any sheet music piece, you would notice that there are always two numbers at the left hand side or after the clef symbol of the staff; one on top of the other.

Elvine Robert

These two numbers are referred to as **time signature** or **meter signature**.

The number at the top specifies how many beats are to be contained in each measure (i.e. between each vertical line called bar) and the number at the bottom specifies the note value for each beats. These beats could be whole (1) note, half (1/2) note, quarter (1/4) note or eight (1/8) note etc.

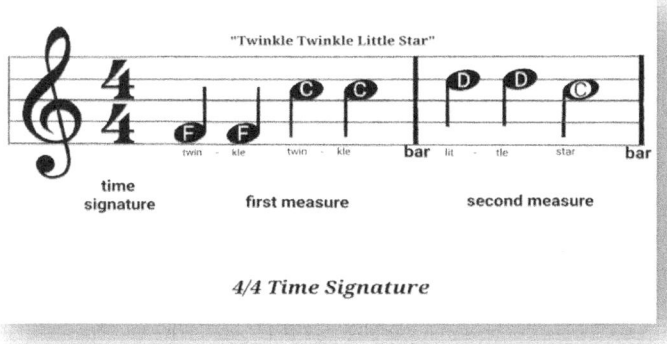

4/4 Time Signature

In the above image, the time signature is 4/4 which means that there are four beats per bar (or in a measure) and each of these beats gets a quarter note. This doesn't limit you to just quarter notes. What it means is that every measure has a total of four quarter note which is also equal to two half note or a whole note.

Beginner's Guide to Playing the Piano Professionally

In the above image, you would also notice that the second measure (or bar) has just three notes of which two are quarter notes and the remaining one is a half note. Since the half note is equal to two quarter note, you would notice that four quarter note to a measure (or bar) has been maintained.

Let's look at another example; a 3/4-time signature. This would mean that there are three beats per bar and that each of these beats gets a quarter note.

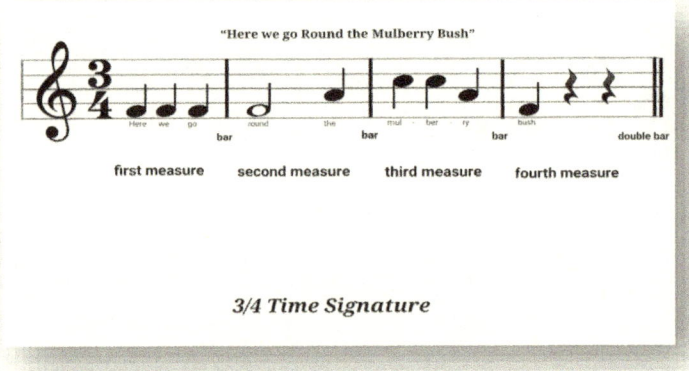

3/4 Time Signature

What if the number at the bottom isn't "4" but "2"? This would mean there are four beats per bar and that each of these beats gets a half note.

Tempo

We've looked at note value; what increases and reduces it. We've also looked at time signature; which tells us how many beats are in a bar and what note value is assigned to each of these beats. Now, "Tempo" is the last missing piece left in order to get the full rhythm of a musical piece.

The tempo or beats per minute (BPM) of a musical piece tells you how **fast** or **slow** such musical piece should be played and is often seen at the **top of a sheet music piece**. A tempo of 60 BPM means that you would play a note every second or 60 notes every minute. Doubling this value to 120 BPM would lead to a double in speed as two notes would be played every second. Italian words like **"Largo"**, **"Moderato"**, **"Allegro"** or **"Presto"** are used to signify common tempos at the top of a musical piece.

Beginner's Guide to Playing the Piano Professionally

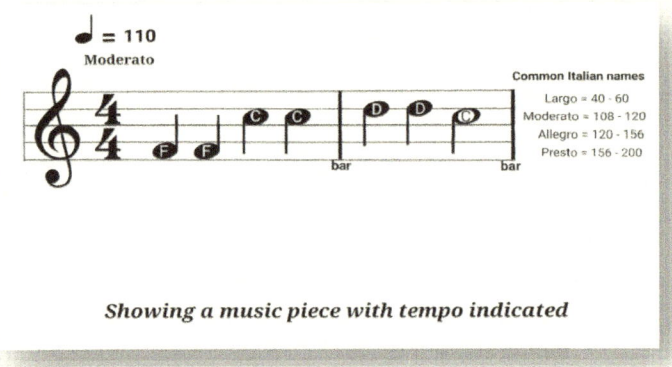

Showing a music piece with tempo indicated

A tool called metronome is used by musicians to maintain tempo while practicing a musical piece. A metronome is like the tic-tac of a clock. It makes a sound distinct sound at equal intervals and can be adjusted to be either slow, fast or very past depending on your chosen tempo.

Key Signature

I think by now; you should have a sketchy knowledge about sight reading. "Sketchy" because you may not yet be able to identify what key a piece of sheet music is written on and also may not understand how the black keys on the piano are represented on a piece of sheet music.

So, what is key signature?

Elvine Robert

A key signature is the number of sharps, flats and sometimes natural symbols used to identify the key of a musical piece. A piece of sheet music with no key signature indicated immediately after the treble clef or bass clef is by default, in the key of C. This is because key C has only white keys with no black keys.

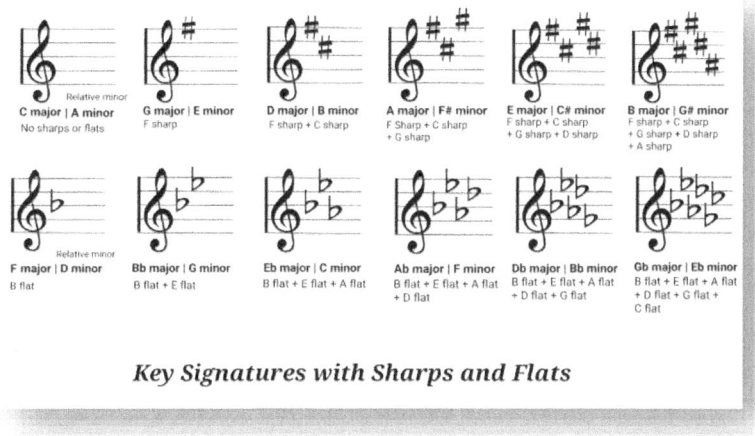

Key Signatures with Sharps and Flats

For other keys with sharps or flats, the key signature tells you to maintain these sharps or flats across the musical piece unless there is a natural symbol to override it. From the above image, wherever the sharp or flat symbol is placed (either on the lines or in the spaces between these lines), the note assigned to that line or space; let's say F, becomes a semitone higher in pitch by adding a sharp (#) to it (i.e. becomes F#) and for flats, becomes a semitone lower by adding a flat (b) to it. Also, you would notice that **A Major** has 3 sharps and these sharps are placed on **space C**, **line D** and **line F**. The notes on these lines would therefore be increased by a semitone since sharps increases notes by a semitone (and flat reduces notes by a semitone). So note C, D and F would then become C#, D# and F#. these notes are seen to be black keys on the piano when playing an A major scale.

If you're having a bit of confusion about why F has a flat and not a sharp, and G has a sharp but not a flat, think no further! The reason is, the key which must be used to represent sharps must not be in the major scale of that key. Another simple way is that all the letters in a major scale must be represented. For example, an F major scale is F – G – A – A# or Bb – C – D – E – F. You would notice that "A" is already represented in the scale, so making use of A# would mean that you would be skipping the letter B in the F major scale, therefore, Bb is correct; making key F a key with a flat.

Apart from key signature, you can also make use of a sharp, a flat or a natural symbol by placing these symbols behind the note in which you want to increase by a half step (sharp) or reduce by a half step (flat) or to bring it back to its natural state by making use of a natural symbol.

Chords in sheet music

By now, you should be able to interpret notes in a sheet music piece. But what if instead of just notes (or melodies), you're faced with chords? It's simple and isn't as complex as you think.

Chords in a sheet music piece are represented with letters or chord names at the top of a staff after each bar line. They are also represented with notes which are stacked on top of each other in a vertical line. These notes are then played together or are played starting from the bottom to the top note (in the case of arpeggios). **Generally, chords are read from the bottom to the top note in a staff.** You may as well see chords as melodic notes that are arranged vertically with all that applies to these melodic notes being maintained when played in harmony (i.e. as a chord).

I'd be making use of sheet music to illustrate techniques, tips and other relevant information in the course of this book.

Chapter Summary

Sight reading is an important skill to acquire as a pianist. In this chapter, we discovered that to learn this skill or know how to read a sheet music piece, you must know some basic keywords such as the staff, notes, pitches and clef. A staff is made up of five lines and four spaces on which a clef sign is drawn. A treble clef drawn on a staff means that notes which are placed on the lines or spaces of these clef would be of high pitches and are played using the right hand. A bass clef drawn on a staff would mean that notes placed on this staff would be of low pitches and these notes are played using the right hand.

Chapter Two

MAJOR, MINOR AND DOMINANT SEVENTH CHORDS

In the level one of this book, we looked at major, minor and diminished triads and how to invert these chords. If you can still recall correctly, we classified chords according to the number of notes held. These are the three note chords (called triads), the four note chords (called sevenths) the five note chord (called ninth), the six note chord (called eleventh) and the seven note chord (called thirteenth).

Since we've already looked at triads; which are three toned chords, in this book, we will be looking at the rest of these chords.

What are seventh chords?

Seventh chords are basically four toned chords. They are like triads, but with an additional seventh note. Just like triads, seventh chords have the Major, Minor, and Diminished chords, plus an additional Dominant chord.

In this chapter, our focus will be on seventh chords, specifically, major, minor and dominant seventh chords.

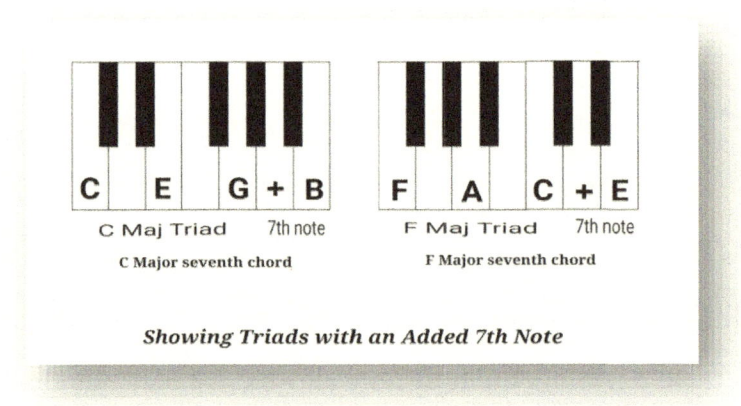

C	E	G + B
C Maj Triad		7th note

C Major seventh chord

F	A	C + E
F Maj Triad		7th note

F Major seventh chord

Showing Triads with an Added 7th Note

The Major Seventh Chord

This is basically a major triad with an added seventh note. In the key of C major, this seventh note would be the B note. In order to get the major seventh chord for the 12 keys on the piano, you must know how to play the major scale for each key. From this major scale you would get the 12 major triad chords of which you then add the seventh tone of the scale.

Elvine Robert

Major Seventh Chords

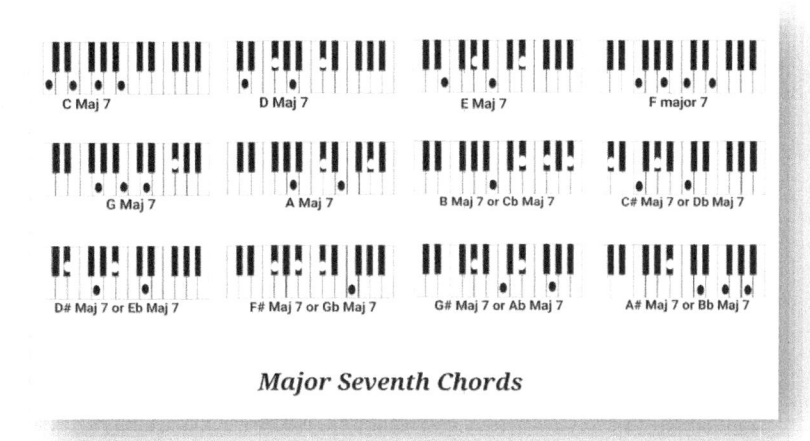

(C Maj 7, D Maj 7, E Maj 7, F major 7, G Maj 7, A Maj 7, B Maj 7 or Cb Maj 7, C# Maj 7 or Db Maj 7, D# Maj 7 or Eb Maj 7, F# Maj 7 or Gb Maj 7, G# Maj 7 or Ab Maj 7, A# Maj 7 or Bb Maj 7)

For example, the major scale of F# is: F#, G#, A#, B, C#, D#, E#, F#. An F# major triad chord would then be F# + A# + C#. In order to make it a major seventh chord, you would add the seventh tone of the scale; which in this case, is E#. Therefore, an F# major seventh chord would be F# + A# + C# + E#.

The dominant seventh chords

As we have learnt from the level one of this series book tagged "The Gateway to Perfection," the V tone of a major scale forms the dominant chord, which almost always leads to the tonic or I chord. For example, in C major, the dominant tone is the G tone. This tone forms a G major triad chord; which is also a dominant chord in the key of C major.

A dominant seventh chord can be formed in three different ways:

1. **By adding a minor 3rd to a major triad chord**

    By adding a minor 3rd to a major triad chord, a dominant seventh chord is formed. For example; in the key of C, a C major triad is C-E-G. Adding a minor 3rd would give you an additional note; this note is seen to be Bb. C dominant seventh chord (C7) would then be C-E-G-Bb. In order to get the dominant seventh chord for the 12 major keys on the piano, you would have to repeat the pattern used above for C major in the remaining keys on the piano by adding a minor 3rd to the twelve (12) major triad on the piano.

2. **By reducing the seventh note of a major seventh chord**

    By reducing the seventh note of a major seventh chord by a semitone, you've successfully formed a dominant seventh chord. In the key of C major, this seventh note is seen to be the B note, and when reduced by a semitone, becomes a Bb note.

Elvine Robert

Dominant Seventh Chords

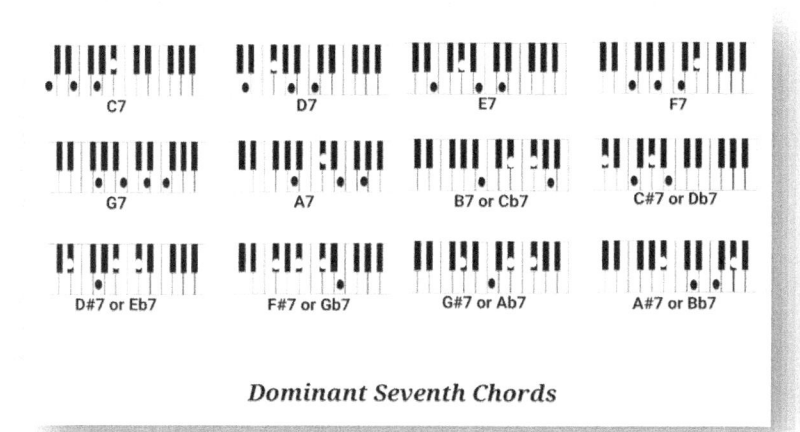

(C7, D7, E7, F7, G7, A7, B7 or Cb7, C#7 or Db7, D#7 or Eb7, F#7 or Gb7, G#7 or Ab7, A#7 or Bb7)

3. By locating the Dominant tone (or V tone) in a Major scale

Another short-cut to playing a dominant seventh chord in any key of your choice is by first locating the dominant tone (also V tone) in the major scale of your chosen key, forming the V major triad chord and then adding the IV tone to this triad. For example, in the key of C major, the V chord is the G major chord and the IV tone is an F tone. By adding the F tone to the G major triad chord, you'd get a G dominant seventh chord (G7).

The Minor Seventh Chords

The minor seventh chord is quite similar to the major and dominant seventh chords. A major seventh chord is a major triad with an added major 3rd and a dominant seventh chord is a major triad with an added minor third. A minor seventh chord is a **minor triad** with an **added minor 3rd** or could be called a dominant chord with the 3rd note flattened.

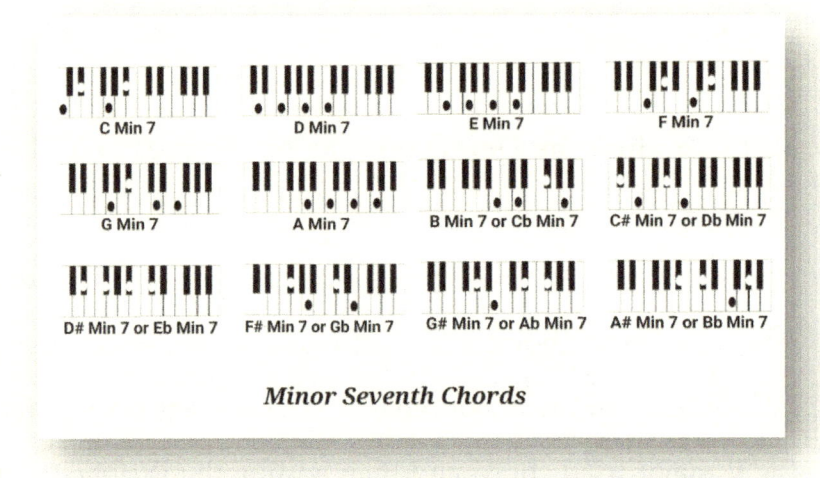

Minor Seventh Chords

In summary, a **major seventh** chord is a **major triad** with an added **major 3rd**, a **dominant seventh** chord is a **major triad** with an **added minor 3rd**, and finally, a **minor seventh** chord is a **minor triad** with an **added minor 3rd**.

Seventh Chords in the Key of C Major

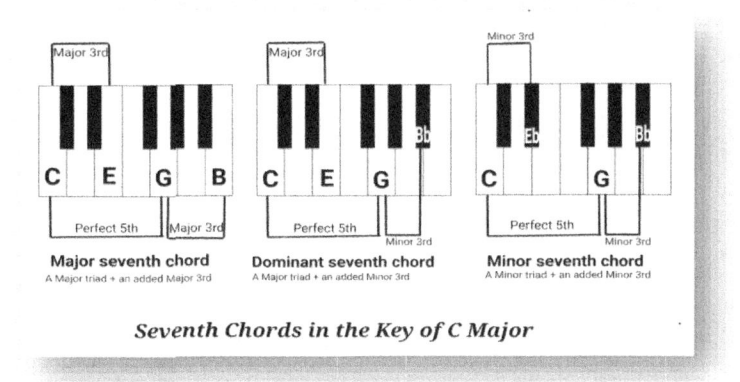

Inversions

In the inversion of seventh chords, you would have the root position, the 1st inversion, the 2nd inversion and finally, the 3rd inversion. Inversion of seventh chords follow the same pattern as triads.

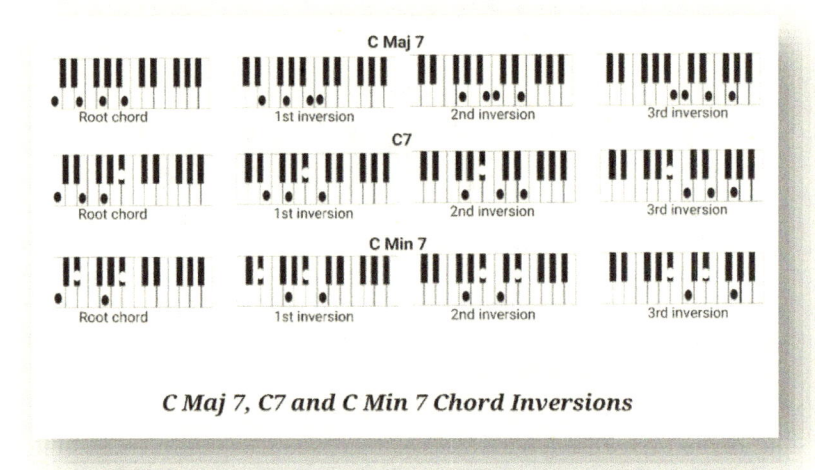

Beginner's Guide to Playing the Piano Professionally

C Maj 7, C7 and C Min 7 Chord Inversions

In the above image, you'd see the inversion for Cmaj7, C7 and Cmin7. To get the inversions of any chord from its root form, you'd take the root note an octave higher to get the 1st inversion, for the 2nd inversion, the root note and the next note in the root chord is taken an octave higher, and finally for the 3rd inversion, the root, the 2nd and 3rd note of the root chord is take an octave higher.

Chapter Summary

Seventh chords are four toned chords which are formed by adding a seventh note to major or minor triad chord. In this seventh chords, we have the major, minor, dominant and diminished seventh chords. Major seventh chords are major triad chords with an added seventh note (or major 3rd), dominant seventh chords are major triads with an added flattened seventh note (or minor 3rd) and minor seventh chords are minor triads with an added flattened seventh note (or minor 3rd).

Chapter Three

MAJOR, MINOR AND DOMINANT SEVENTH CHORD PROGRESSIONS

In the previous chapter, we learnt how to form major, minor and dominant seventh chords. In this chapter, we'll be looking at how to make use of these chords to play different chord progressions.

Every note on a major scale corresponds to either a major, minor or diminished chord. I have explained this concept using triads. The image below will give you each note on a major scale and its corresponding seventh chord.

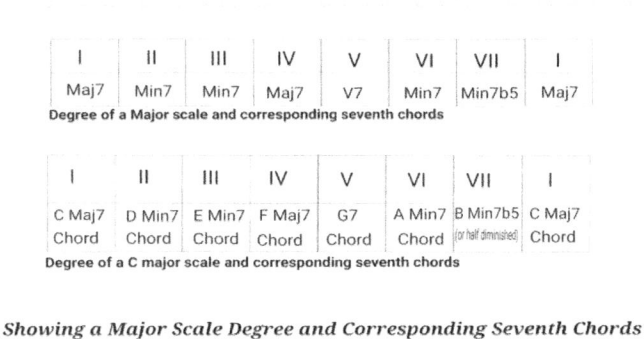

I	II	III	IV	V	VI	VII	I
Maj7	Min7	Min7	Maj7	V7	Min7	Min7b5	Maj7

Degree of a Major scale and corresponding seventh chords

I	II	III	IV	V	VI	VII	I
C Maj7 Chord	D Min7 Chord	E Min7 Chord	F Maj7 Chord	G7 Chord	A Min7 Chord	B Min7b5 (or half diminished)	C Maj7 Chord

Degree of a C major scale and corresponding seventh chords

Showing a Major Scale Degree and Corresponding Seventh Chords

We'll be looking at the following chord progressions:
1. 1-4-1-5-1,
2. 1-4-5-4-1,
3. 2-5-1,
4. 6-2-5-1,
5. 3-6-2-5-1,
6. and the 7-3-6-2-5-1.

Other chord progressions are the 5-1, 1-5, and the 1-4 chord progressions.

You've already learnt how to play these chord progressions using triad, now, we'll be playing this same chord progressions, but instead of triads, we'll be making use of seventh chords.

1. The I-IV-I-V-I (1-4-1-5-1) Chord Progression

In this chord progression, we'd be making use of just the major seventh chords. To get these chords, you'd have to follow the pattern used for forming major seventh chords for the I, IV and V tone of a major scale in the chapter two of this book. By simply adding a major 3rd to the I and IV triads you've formed their major seventh chords. For the V chord; which is a natural dominant chord, you'd add a minor 3rd to its major triad.

Showing the I-IV-I-V-I Chord Progression in C Major

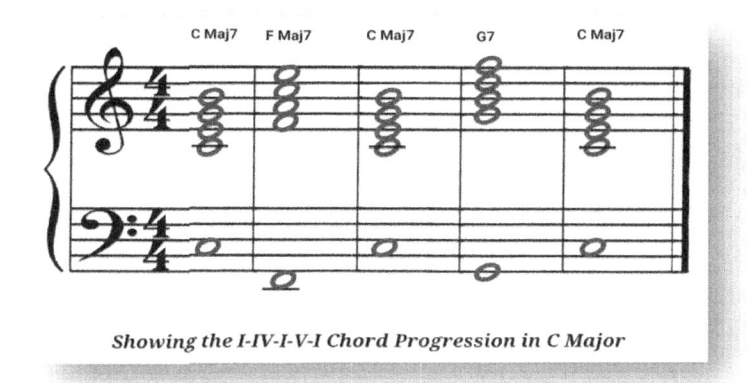

Playing this chord progression in their root form may become rather challenging for fast tempos and this can only be solved by making use of inversions. Chords may be used in their root form in a chord progression if it fits perfectly to the kind of sound you're looking for when composing a song. Introducing inversions to your piano playing skill not only makes fast tempo songs easier to play, but also brings in more dynamic to your music, as well as making the piano more fun, exciting and entertaining.

By simply playing the root of the I chord, the 2nd inversion of the IV chord and finally, the first (or second) inversion of the V chord, you would be able to transit easily from one chord to the other in this chord progression.

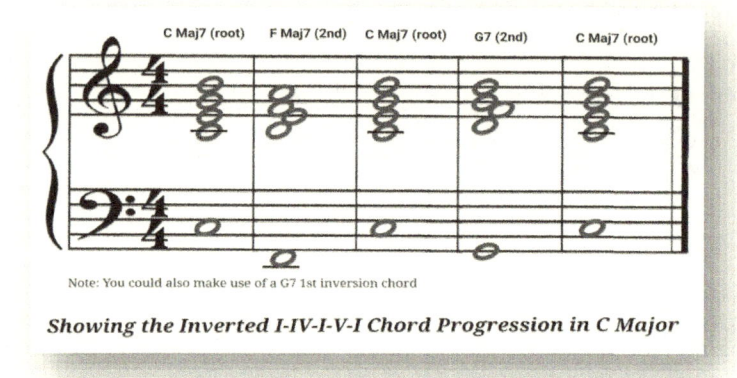

Beginner's Guide to Playing the Piano Professionally

Showing the Inverted I-IV-I-V-I Chord Progression in C Major

Note: Inversions of seventh chords may not be as easy as you may have thought it would, but with some time and effort, you'd be able to play these inversions with ease.

2. I-IV-V-IV-I Chord Progression

This chord progression is similar to the previous as the same I, IV and V chords were used for this chord progression.

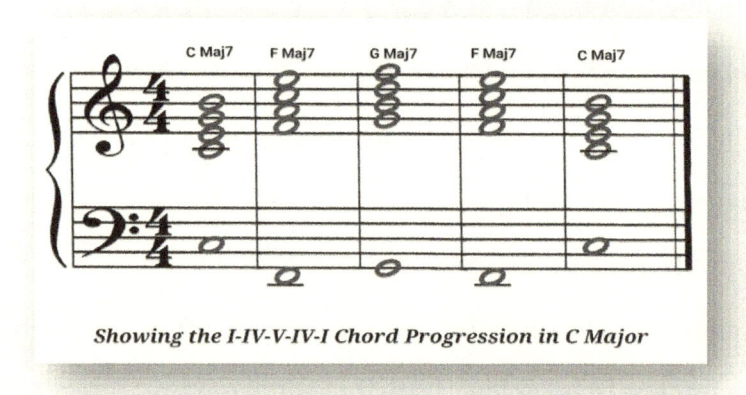

Showing the I-IV-V-IV-I Chord Progression in C Major

Elvine Robert

Showing the Inverted I-IV-V-IV-I Chord Progression in C Major

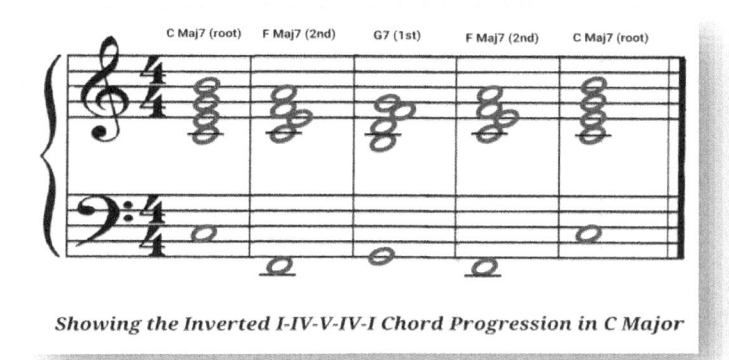

Note: The V-I, I-V and the I-IV are contained in the above progressions.

3. The II-V-I Chord Progression

As earlier mentioned, each tone of a scale has a specific chord it forms. For this chord progression, the II tone forms a minor seventh chord, the V tone, a dominant seventh chord and then to the I chord, which is a major seventh chord.

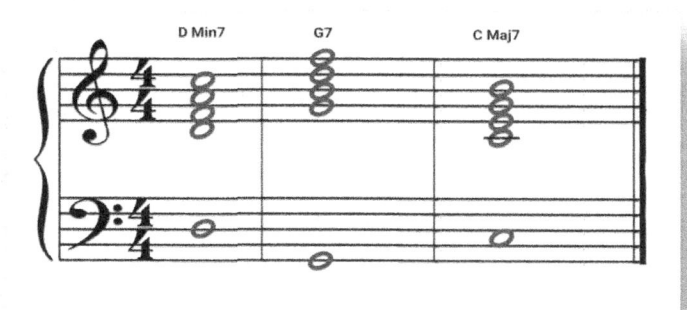

Showing the II-V-I Chord Progression in C Major

By simply introducing inversion to this chord progression, the progression is played a lot smoother.

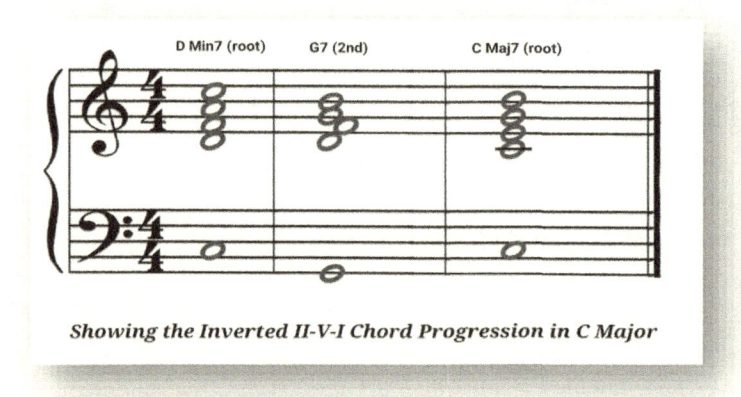

Showing the Inverted II-V-I Chord Progression in C Major

i. **Another approach to the II-V-I chord progression**

In the level one of this book, we also looked at this chord progression. If you can recall, the II chord, which is a minor chord was played (using triad) and then to the V back to the I chord. This chord progression was altered such that we played a II major triad instead of the minor. Therefore, the II major triad was serving as a dominant chord to the V chord, but because the V chord isn't the tonic or I chord, this II major triad was referred to as a secondary dominant chord.

Elvine Robert

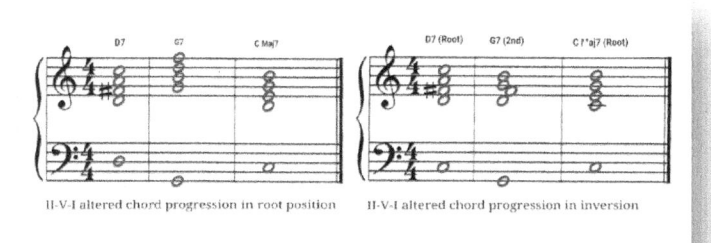

Showing the II-V-I Altered Chord Progression in C Major

In the case of seventh chords, this alteration is clearer as instead of playing a II minor seventh chord, you'd play a II dominant seventh chord. In the key of C major, this chord progression would be D7-G7-Cmaj7 instead of Dmin7-G7-Cmaj7.

Secondary Dominant	Dominant	Secondary Dominant	Dominant
C7	F7	F#7 or Gb7	B7
C#7 or Db7	F#7 or Gb7	G7	C7
D7	G7	G#7 or Ab7	C#7 or Db7
D#7 or Eb7	G#7 or Ab7	A7	D7
E7	A7	A#7 or Bb7	D#7 or Eb7
F7	Bb7	G7	E7

Showing the 12 "II-V" Secondary Dominant Relationship on the Piano

Beginner's Guide to Playing the Piano Professionally

4. The VI-II-V-I Chord Progression

This chord is simply the combination of the II-V-I chord progression plus an extra chord; the VI chord, which is a minor seventh chord.

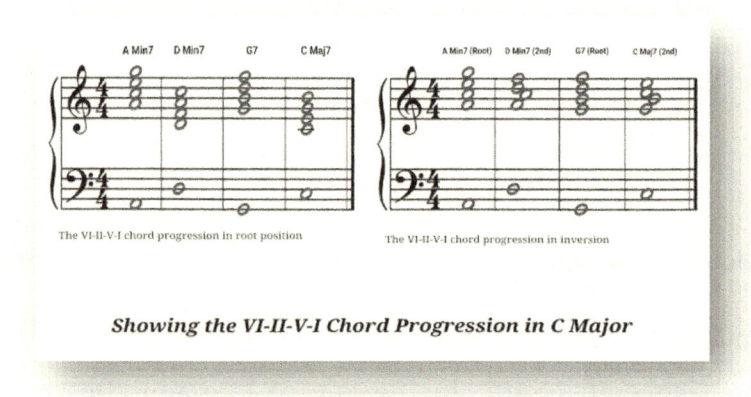

The VI-II-V-I chord progression in root position

The VI-II-V-I chord progression in inversion

Showing the VI-II-V-I Chord Progression in C Major

Try playing the VI-II-V-I chord progression (from the above image) in their root form and when inversion is applied to the II and I chord of this chord progression. You'd notice how much better and easier this chord progression is, when inversions are used.

Inversions are used by pianist or musicians to transit from one chord to the closest available chord and for harmonizing melodies by making certain notes in a chord be at the top or bottom of that chord.

i. A second approach to the VI-II-V-I chord progression

Like I earlier said, every note on a major scale has a chord it forms. From all these chords, the V chord is the only dominant chord which leads to the I chord. Any other chord which act as a dominant chord but doesn't lead to the I chord are referred to as secondary dominant chords.

In this approach, we'll play a VI dominant seventh chord instead of the VI minor chord. An example of this alteration using C major would be A7-D7-G7-Cmaj7 instead of Amin7-Dmin7-G7-Cmaj7. Like I mentioned in the level one of this book, this chord progression is commonly started with the I chord. In C major, this chord progression would be Cmaj7-A7-D7-G7-Cmaj7. This chord progression is commonly seen at the end of various Gospel music.

Beginner's Guide to Playing the Piano Professionally

The VI-II-V-I altered chord progression in root position *The VI-II-V-I altered chord progression in inversion*

Showing the VI-II-V-I Altered Chord Progression in C Major

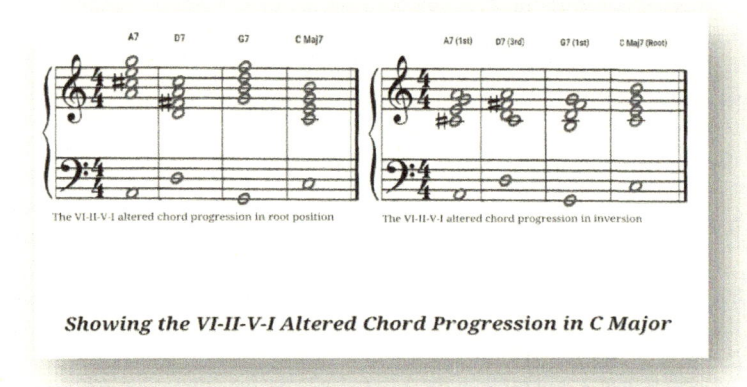

Note: this altered chord progression has two secondary dominant chords; the VI and II chord. VI chord acts as a dominant chord to the II chord and the II chord act as a dominant chord to the V chord.

5. The III-VI-II-V-I Chord Progression

Just like the trend has been; following the circle of fifths, this chord progression is gotten by adding a III minor chord to the "VI-II-V-I" chord progression. This gives you the III-VI-II-V-I chord progression. In the key of C major, this chord progression would be Emin7-Amin7-Dmin7-G7-Cmaj7.

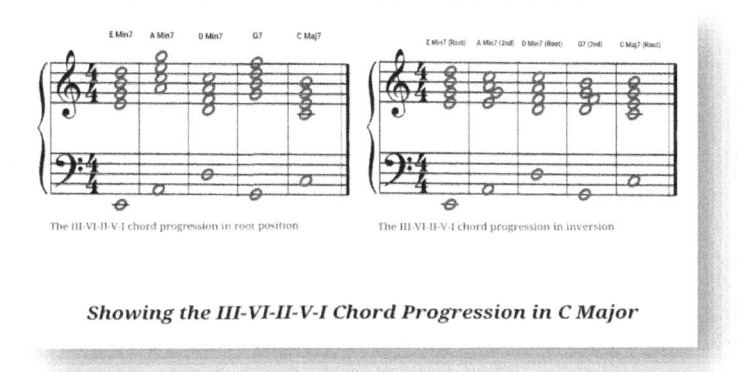

Showing the III-VI-II-V-I Chord Progression in C Major

i. Another approach to the III-VI-II-V-I chord progression

Just like we've altered the VI and II minor chords to form dominant seventh chords, we'll also be altering this III minor chord to form a dominant seventh chord.

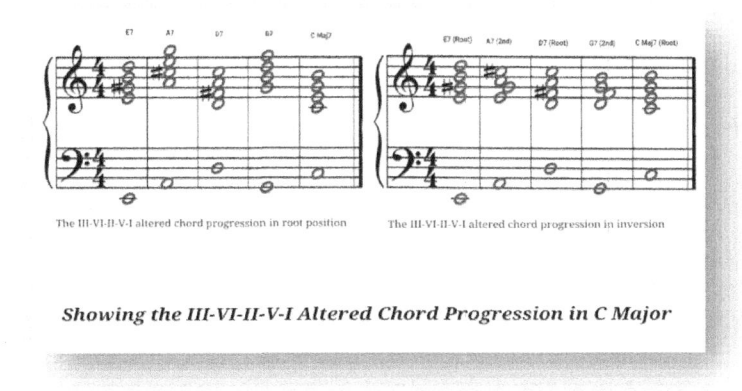

Showing the III-VI-II-V-I Altered Chord Progression in C Major

Let me use this opportunity to make clearer what secondary dominant chords are, but this time, will be making use of C major to illustrate it.

I think by now, it's no doubt that every key has, let's say "a natural dominant chord", which almost always leads to the tonic or I chord. This would be from the G chord to the I chord in the key of C. When you look closely at the II-V-I altered chord progression (where the II dominant chord was used), which in the key of C major is D7-G7-Cmaj7, you would notice that there is a relationship between these chords; D7 and G7 are both dominant chords. Let's see it from this view: a dominant chord always leads to the tonic, so if D7 is a dominant chord, then G7 (or Gmaj7) should be the tonic or resting chord. Unfortunately, this isn't so in this case, as Gmaj7 isn't the resting chord of C major, but it is the resting chord of G major. When you go ahead and look at G major scale, G-A-B-C-D-E-F#-G, you'd notice that the V chord (a natural dominant chord) is actually a D chord. So therefore, D7 is a natural dominant chord leading to the Gmaj7 resting chord in the key of G major. In reality, we play this same D7 chord to G chord (now a G7 and not Gmaj7) so therefore, D7 is a secondary dominant chord because it is a dominant chord in the key of G, but because in C major, G isn't the tonic or resting chord, it is referred to as a secondary dominant chord. This pattern also applies to the III dominant seventh chord and the VI dominant seventh chord.

12-Bar Blues Chord Progression

I am pretty sure that this isn't your first time of seeing this phrase. This chord progression is common almost in all styles of music including the Blues, Gospel and Jazz.

This chord progression uses only the primary chord of a major scale on the piano. These chords are the I, IV and V chords, which in the key of C major, are; the C major, F major and G major chords respectively. However, when it comes to the 12-bar Blues chord progression, only the dominant of these chords are used. This would be the I, IV and V dominant chords, which are the C7, F7 and G7 chords in the key of C major. This gives it the bluesy sound we need.

In playing this dominant chords you could choose to omit the I tone for each chord, that is, if you are already playing this tone with your left hand. In cases of improvising, you would

Beginner's Guide to Playing the Piano Professionally

play this 12-bar blues chord progression with the left hand while improvising on the right hand.

Since we already know the chords used for this chord progression; which are the I7, IV7 and the V7 chords, we'll be looking at how these chords are used in the 12-bar blues chord progression.

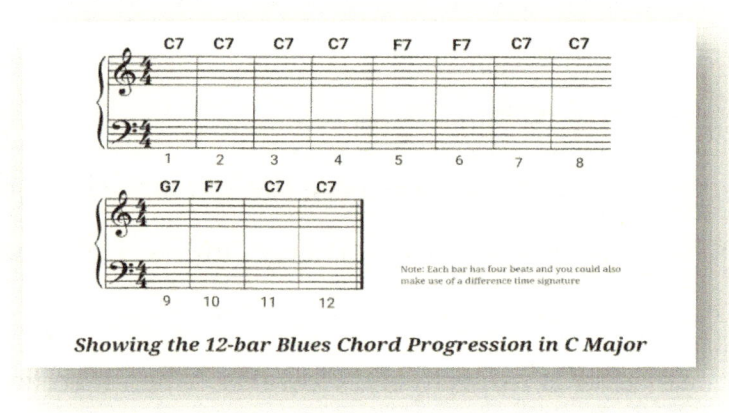

Showing the 12-bar Blues Chord Progression in C Major

Note: In playing the above 12-bar blues chord progression, the closest inversion of these chords are played.

From the above image, you would notice that each bar in this 12-bar blues chord progression has a number of 4 beats. This gives you a total number of 48 beats for the 12-bar blues chord progression. This chord progression requires you to move from C7 to F7, back to C7, then to G7, to F7 and back to C7.

Elvine Robert

Since the chords used for this chord progression are all dominant chords, including the C chord, you'd discover that this chord progression can continue forever since there is no resting chord.

Chapter Summary

This chapter was all about chord progressions. The major, minor and dominant seventh chords were used for these chord progressions. We also looked at how the dominant seventh chords are used in chord progressions following the circle of fifths and finally how these dominant chords are used in the 12-bar blues chord progression.

Chapter Four

DIMINISHED SEVENTH, MAJOR SIXTH AND MINOR SIXTHS CHORDS

In the previous chapter, we looked at different chord progressions including progressions following the circle of fifth pattern. The 7-3-6-2-5-1 (or VII-III-VI-II-V-I) chord progression was skipped in **chapter three** because we are yet to learn the VII (7) chord; which is a diminished seventh chord. In this chapter, we'll be looking closely at the diminished seventh chords and a different kind of chord called the sixth chords.

The Diminished Seventh Chords

As we earlier learnt, the term **"diminished"** means **"made smaller"**. When a **minor** or **perfect interval** is made smaller by a **semitone** or by **half a step**, it is referred to as a **diminished interval**.

In order to form a diminished triad, you would simply just reduce the fifth tone of a minor triad by a semitone. You'd

Beginner's Guide to Playing the Piano Professionally

notice that this diminished chord has an interval pattern of a minor 3rd on a minor 3rd (minor 3rd + minor 3rd).

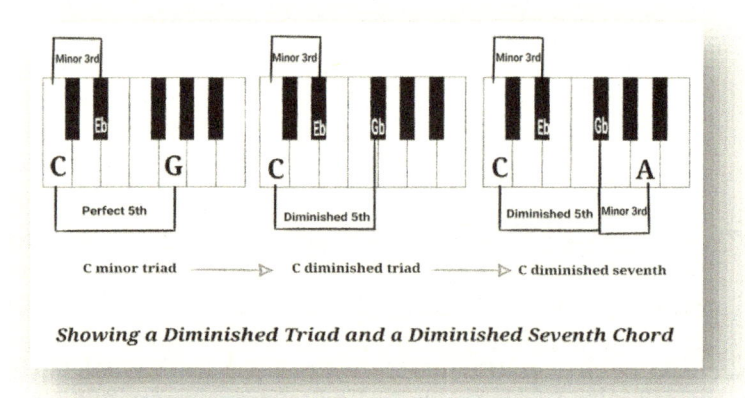

Showing a Diminished Triad and a Diminished Seventh Chord

In forming diminished seventh chords, you'd simply add another **minor 3rd** to a **diminished triad**. This gives you an interval pattern of three minor 3rd (**minor 3rd + minor 3rd + minor 3rd**).

Although, the major, minor and dominant seventh chords each forms twelve (12) different chords on the piano, the diminished seventh chord in a way, also forms twelve (12) chords on the piano, but when you take a close look at these chords, you'd notice that this chords aren't so different from each other. In actuality, we only have three (3) groups of diminished seventh chords on the piano from which the twelve diminished chords are seen to fall under. These three groups are based on these diminished seventh chords sharing the same notes.

1. **In the first group**, we have the C dim7, Eb/D# dim7, F#/Gb dim7, and A dim7 chords.
2. **In the second group**, we have the D dim7, F dim7, G#/Ab dim7 and the B/Cb dim7 chords.
3. **For the third and last group**, we have the C#/Db dim7, E dim7, G dim7 and A#/Bb dim7 chords.

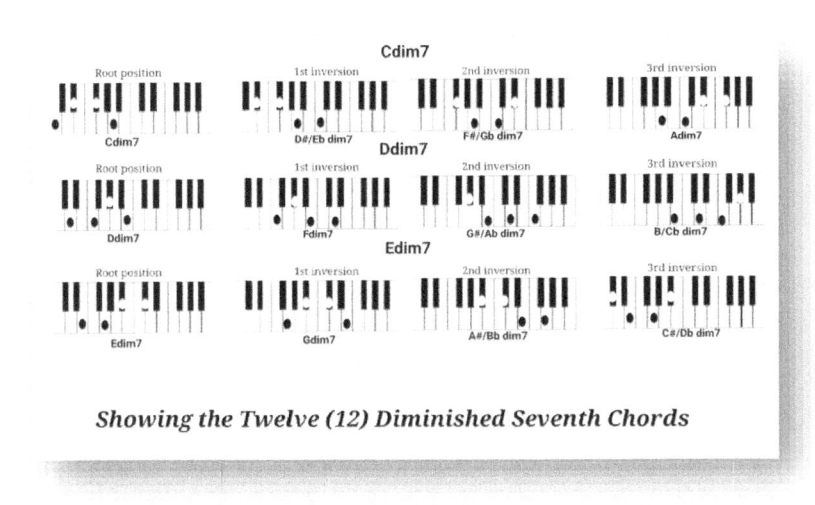

Showing the Twelve (12) Diminished Seventh Chords

Take a chord from one of these groups. Try playing this chord and its inversions and note how the inversions corresponds to other chords in that same group.

The Half Diminished Seventh Chords

There's another diminished chord called the half diminished seventh chord, which is the chord formed on the VII (7) tone of a major scale. This chord is called half diminished seventh chord because, unlike diminished seventh chords, this chord has a major 3rd as one of its intervals. **Half diminished chords are formed by the interval pattern; minor 3rd + minor 3rd + major 3rd**.

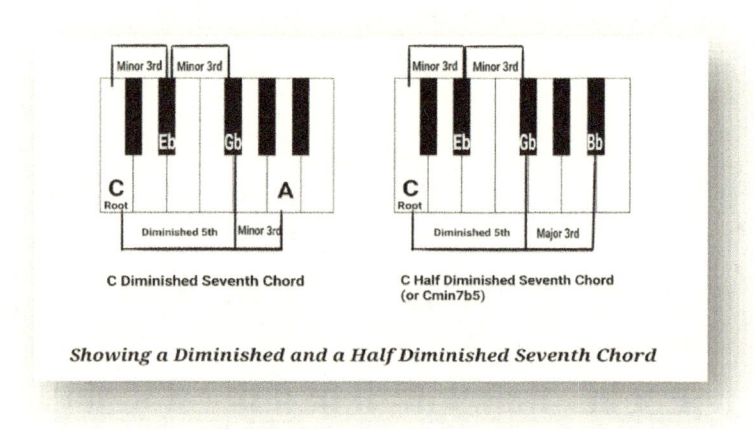

C Diminished Seventh Chord

C Half Diminished Seventh Chord (or Cmin7b5)

Showing a Diminished and a Half Diminished Seventh Chord

If you're wondering why the VII (7) tone of a major scale forms a half diminished seventh chord and not the diminished seventh chord, then let me to take you a step or two backward to make this clear.

Since we started looking at seventh chords, we've covered the major, minor and dominant seventh chords. For better understanding, let me make use of C major to illustrate this concept. A C major scale is C-D-E-F-G-A-B-C. These tones form a major, minor, dominant and diminished seventh chords. Only tones in a C major scale are used in forming these chords. Other chords formed with tones outside this C major scale could be referred to as altered chords. For example, using the D7 chord in the II-V-I dominant chord progression instead of a D Min7.

When you look at a dim7 (specifically a Bdim7) chord, you'd notice that we are having a note which is not on the C major scale, making this chord to not fit into the chord formed by the VII (7) tone of a C major scale.

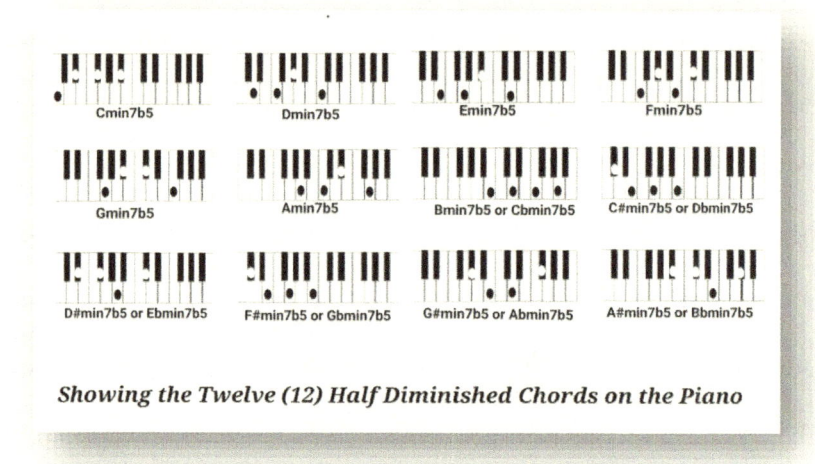

Beginner's Guide to Playing the Piano Professionally

Cmin7b5	Dmin7b5	Emin7b5	Fmin7b5
Gmin7b5	Amin7b5	Bmin7b5 or Cbmin7b5	C#min7b5 or Dbmin7b5
D#min7b5 or Ebmin7b5	F#min7b5 or Gbmin7b5	G#min7b5 or Abmin7b5	A#min7b5 or Bbmin7b5

Showing the Twelve (12) Half Diminished Chords on the Piano

A half diminished seventh chord can also be seen as a minor seventh chord with a flattened 5th (Min7 b5).

Major and Minor Sixth Chords

Just like the seventh chords are formed by adding the seventh note, these chords are formed by adding the sixth note.

A **major sixth** chord is formed by adding the **sixth degree** (or note) to a **major triad**, while a **minor sixth** chord is formed by adding the **sixth degree** (or note) to a **minor triad**. In C major, the sixth degree is the A note. The C major sixth chord would then be a C major triad (C-E-G) and an added sixth note (A), which gives you **C-E-G-A**. A minor sixth chord would be a minor triad (C-Eb-G) and an added sixth note (A), which gives you **C-Eb-G-A**.

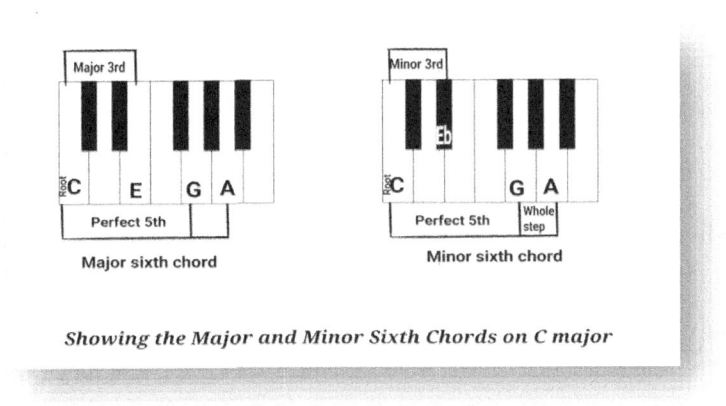

Showing the Major and Minor Sixth Chords on C major

This major and minor sixth chords are found to have a relationship with the minor seventh and half diminished seventh chords respectively. For example, a **C major sixth chord (C6)** is found to have the same notes as an **A minor seventh (Amin7)** and a **C minor sixth chord (Cmin6)** is found to have the same notes as an **A half diminished seventh chord (or Amin7b5)**. For clarity, let's look at this C6 and how it relates with Amin7 and also how Cmin6 relates with Amin7b5.

For the C6 and Amin7, the first thing you should take note of is how Amin is the relative minor key of C major. When you play this Amin7, you would notice that the 1st inversion would give you a C6 chord. In the 12 keys on the piano, the chords formed on the relative minor of a major key are always seen to be equivalent to the sixth chord formed on that major key. You could also say that the minor seventh chord formed on the sixth degree (or tone) of a major scale is equivalent to the sixth major chord formed on the 1st degree (or tone). **Therefore, a major sixth chord is said to be equivalent to a minor seventh chord.**

MAJOR SIXTH CHORD	MINOR SEVENTH CHORDS
C6	Amin7
C#6 or Db6	A#min7 or Bbmin7
D6	Bmin7
D#6 or Eb6	Cmin7
E6	C#min7 or Dbmin7
F6	Dmin7
F#6/Gb6	D#min7 or Ebmin7
G6	Emin7
G#6/Ab6	Fmin7
A6	F#min7 or Gbmin7
A#6 or Bb6	Gmin7
B6	G#min7 or Abmin7

Showing the Relationship Between Major Sixth and Minor Seventh Chords

When it comes to the relationship between Cmin6 and Amin7b5, there is a little bit of variation. Just like the explanation I gave for C6 and Amin7, the only little variation is, the C6 chord has it 3rd note flattened to give a Cmin6 chord and the Amin7 chord has its 5th note flattened to give an Amin7b5 (also a half diminished chord). In reality, these notes that are flattened are seen to be the same, **therefore a minor sixth chord is said to be equal to a half diminished seventh chord.**

MINOR SIXTH CHORDS	HALF DIMINISHED SEVENTH CHORDS
Cm6	Amin7b5
C#m6 or Dbm6	A#min7b5 or Bbmin7b5
Dm6	Bmin7b5
D#m6 or Ebm6	Cmin7b5
Em6	C#min7b5 or Ebmin7b5
Fm6	Dmin7b5
F#m6 or Gbm6	D#min7b5 or Ebmin7b5
Gm6	Emin7b5
G#m6 or Abm6	Fmin7b5
Am6	F#min7b5 or Gbmin7b5
A#m6 or Bbm6	Gmin7b5
Bm6	G#min7b5 or Abmin7b5

Showing the Relationship Between Minor Sixth and Half Diminished Seventh Chords

Chapter Summary

The sixth chords are triads with an added sixth note. They are divided into major and minor sixth chords. A major and a minor sixth chords are found to be equal to a minor seventh and a half diminished seventh chords respectively. The diminished seventh chord is formed by adding a minor 3rd to a diminished triad and when a major 3rd is added to a diminished triad, it is referred to as a half diminished seventh chord.

Chapter Five

MAJOR SIXTH, MINOR SIXTH AND DIMINISHED CHORD PROGRESSIONS

In this chapter, we'll be looking at major sixth, minor sixth and diminished seventh chord progression. Remember that the major and minor sixth chords are equal to the minor seventh and half diminished seventh chords. Wherever you play a minor seventh chord or a half diminished chord, you've "technically" played a major and minor sixth chord. For now, I'd leave you to experiment with these sixth chords.

If by now, you're still finding it difficult to apply the chords we've learnt so far, do not bother yourself as we'll be looking at the application of these chords (plus other chords we'll be learning later) in various songs before this series comes to an end.

In chapter three, we looked at different chord progressions, and also chord progressions following the circle of fifth chart.

We skipped the VIII-III-VI-II-V-I chord progression because we had not learnt how to play the diminished seventh chords. We'll be looking at this chord progression, but before we do, let's look at how this diminished chord is applied to other chord progressions.

The Diminished Chord in the 2-5-1 Chord Progression

We have already looked at this chord progression using seventh chords and also have looked at how this chord progression is altered using the dominant II chord to replace the minor II chord. Now, we'll be looking at how diminished chords can be used in this chord progression.

The secondary diminished chord

Since we already know that the diminished chord usually takes you to the tonic, just like the secondary dominant chord, a diminished chord which leads to another chord that is not the tonic is referred to as a secondary diminished chord. Using C major, F#dim7 (or IV# dim7) is a diminished chord whose tonic is a G major chord, but since G major isn't the tonic of C major, this chord is referred to as a secondary diminished chord.

Showing the II-V-I Chord Progression using Diminished Chords

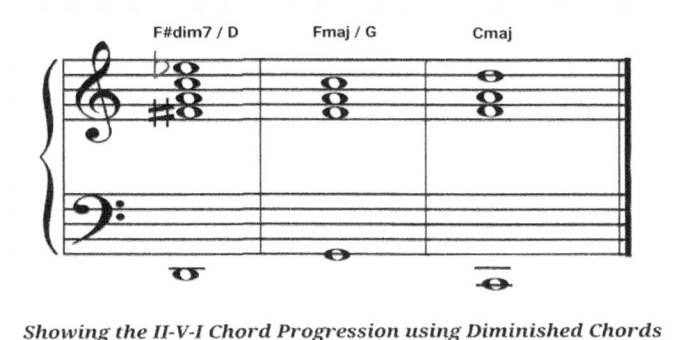

In playing this II-V-I chord progression you'd replace the II min7 with a IV# dim7 chord. In C major, this would be an F# dim7 chord to G7 and then to C maj7. In addition to this alteration you may as well play a IV maj7 triad with the V bass to replace the V7 chord. In the key of C, this would be an F maj triad with G as bass. Also, you could as well decide to use a half diminished seventh chord to replace the diminished seventh chord. it all depends on the sound you're looking for.

Beginner's Guide to Playing the Piano Professionally

Showing the II-V-I Chord Progression Using Half Diminished Chords

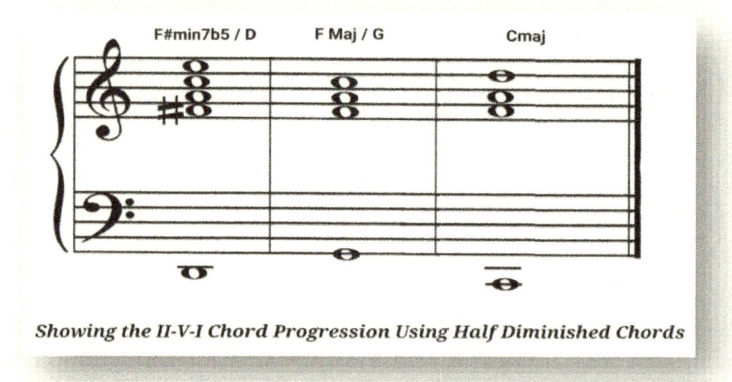

The Diminished Seventh Chord as Passing Chord

The diminished seventh chord can be used as a puller or a passing chord to another chord. In the key of C, this chord can be used as a passing chord to Dmin and Emin. For example, you'd play, let's say a II-V-I chord progression but starting from C maj7 to C# dim7 and then to Dmin7-G7-Cmaj7 chord progression.

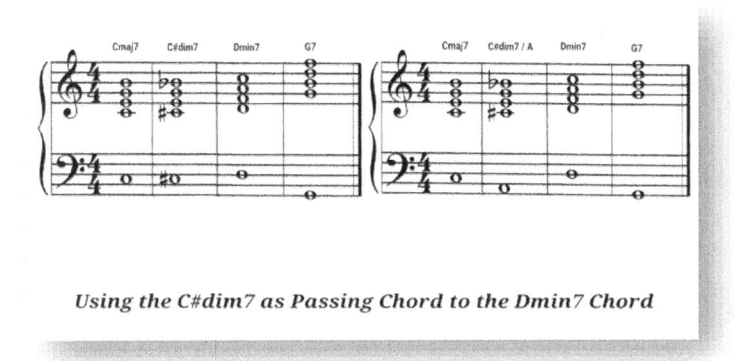

Using the C#dim7 as Passing Chord to the Dmin7 Chord

In the case of using it as a passing chord to Emin, you'd play this chord progression C-Ebdim7-Emin-A7-D7-G7-Cmaj7.

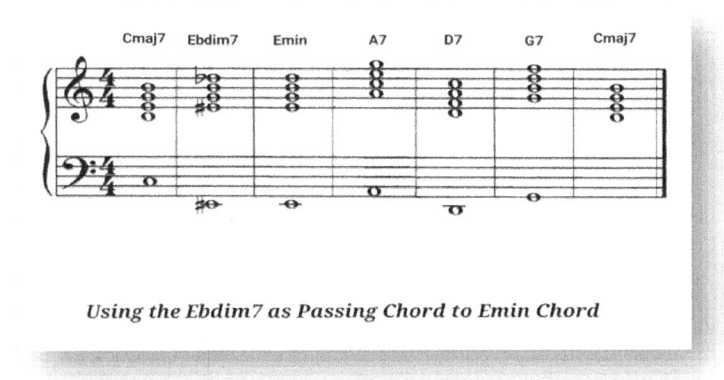

Using the Ebdim7 as Passing Chord to Emin Chord

Since a VI chord also leads to the II chord, you could play a C#dim7 chord but with a VI note as bass.

The VII-III-VI-II-V-I Chord Progression

This chord progression is gotten by simply adding a VII chord to a "III-VI-II-V-I" chord progression. This VII seventh chord as earlier stated, is a half diminished chord. Using C major as an example, this chord progression would be Bmin7b5-Emin7-Amin7-Dmin7-G7-Cmaj7. You could also alter these chords to get all dominant chords excluding the VII chord and the I chord. We'll be altering some of these chords to get Bmin7b5-E5-Amin7-D7-G7-Cmaj7.

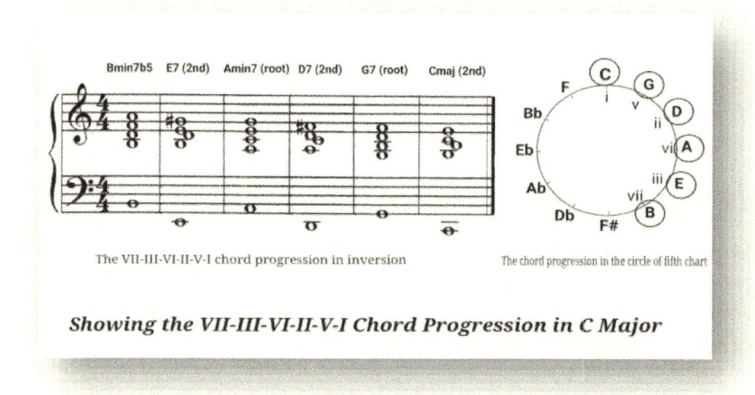

Showing the VII-III-VI-II-V-I Chord Progression in C Major

Diminished Seventh chords in Gospel Progression

A very common Gospel progression is a chord progression that moves from a diminished seventh to a dominant seventh chord. This progression is used when the piano is played during a church sermon. In C major, this is simply moving from Cdim7 to C7 while maintaining the same C bass note.

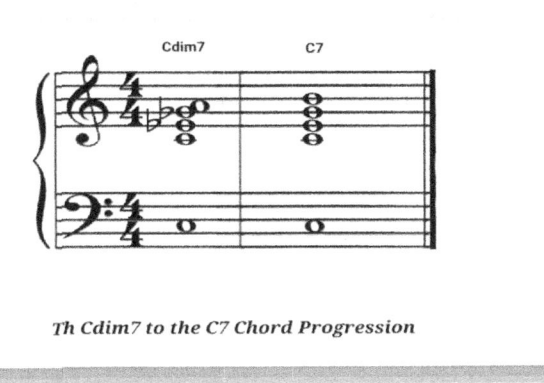

Th Cdim7 to the C7 Chord Progression

Another common Gospel progression is when there is a diminished seventh chord between a IV dominant chord and a I major chord. In the key of C major, this would be F7-F#dim7-Cmaj/G.

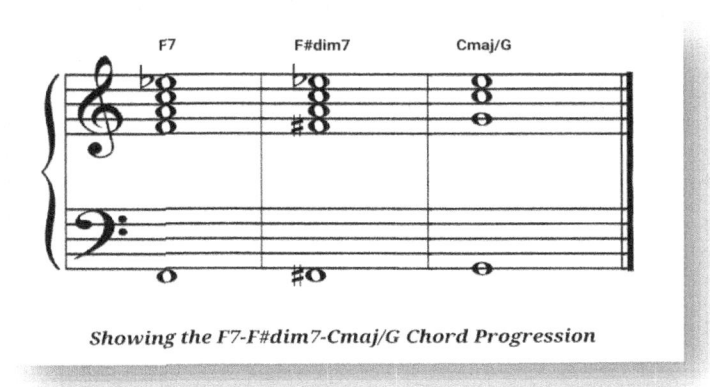

Showing the F7-F#dim7-Cmaj/G Chord Progression

Taking a close look at this chord progression, you would notice that the bass note of this chord progression was ascending by a semitone from F to F# and then to G.

In playing the piano, never you stop practicing, as the more time you give to practicing, the more you discover more hidden secrets about the piano.

Chapter Summary

In this chapter, we saw that a diminished chord can be used in varieties of ways when it comes to chord progressions. They can be used as passing chords, such that they act as a puller to other chords. We also looked at secondary diminished chords, which are diminished chords that leads to another chord which isn't the tonic. The diminished chords are also found to be useful in Gospel chord progression and finally in the VII-III-VI-II-V-I.

Chapter Six

MAJOR, MINOR, AND DOMINANT NINTH CHORDS

We've looked at the three-toned chords (or triads) and also looked at the four-toned chords (or sevenths). In this chapter, we'll be looking at the five-toned chords or ninth chords.

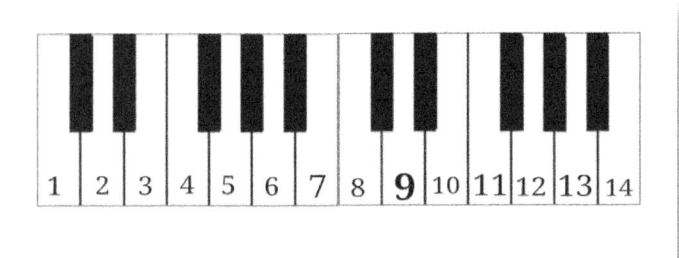

Showing the Ninth Tone on C Major

In forming, seventh chords, we simply added the seventh (7th) tone to a triad. In order to form ninth chords, we'll have to add a **ninth** (9th) tone a **seventh chord.**

The Major Ninth Chords

In forming these chords, you'd simply add a **ninth** (9th) tone to a **major seventh chord**. This gives you a major ninth chord. In the key of C major, this would mean adding the D tone to a Cmaj7.

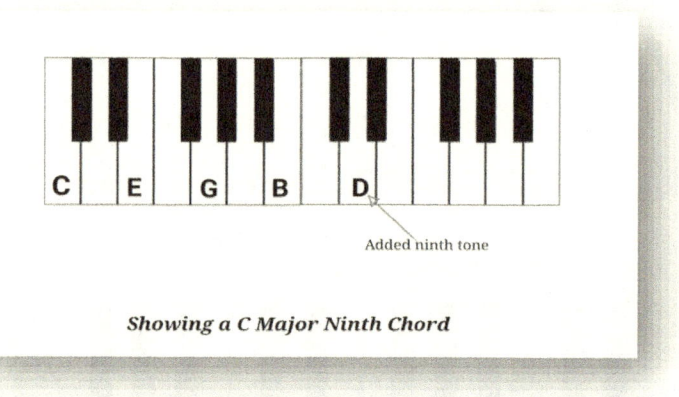

Added ninth tone

Showing a C Major Ninth Chord

Generally, if you know how to play the major scale of the 12 major keys on the piano (which I believe you do), you would be able to easily form this major ninth chords on the piano.

In playing the major ninth chords, I most times prefer playing the added ninth tone an octave lower, such that this tone is embedded in the major ninth chord.

Elvine Robert

Added ninth tone

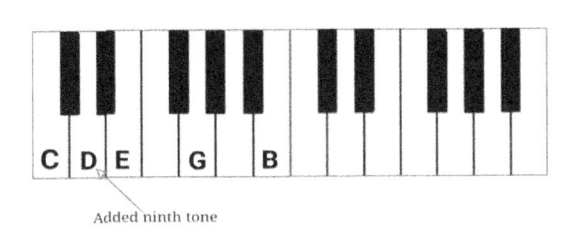

The Ninth Tone Embedded in the Major Ninth Chord

You could also play the major ninth chords by separating the root tone (or keynote), such that you would play this keynote as bass and the rest of the chord as a seventh chord.

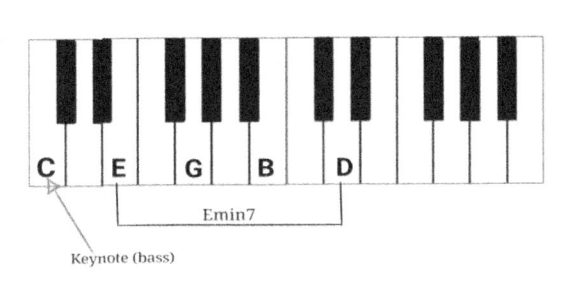

Keynote (bass) — Emin7

Playing the C Major Ninth Chord by Separating the Root Tone

For example, in C major, this would mean playing a C bass note with an Emin7 chord as shown in the above image.

Try playing this major ninth chord for the 12 major keys on the piano. This you can do by first knowing how to play the major scale of any key, of which the major ninth chord you wish to form. A major triad is formed by taking the 1st, 3rd and 5th note of that major scale. Adding the 7th tone to this triad, gives you a seventh chord and adding the ninth tone, gives you a major ninth chord.

Minor Ninth Chords

Just like major ninth chords, minor ninth chords are simply **minor seventh chords** with an added **ninth tone**. You could also see these minor ninth chords as a **keynote** with an added **relative major seventh** chord of this keynote. For example, in C minor, the relative major key is Eb major. So by playing the key note, which is the C note and an Eb major seventh chord, you've succeeded in forming a C minor ninth chord.

Showing a C Minor Ninth Chord

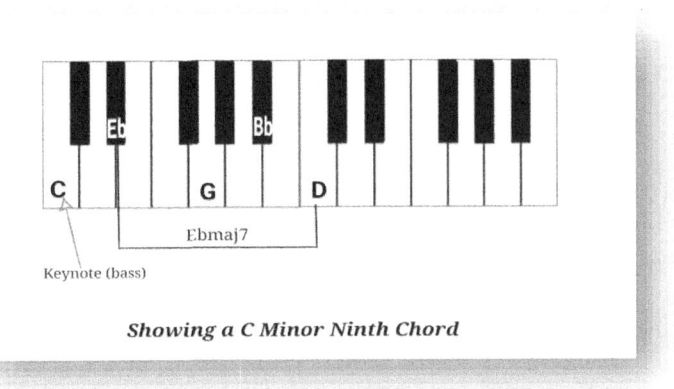

To form an A minor ninth chord, you'd first of all find the relative major of A minor. This would be a C major. So to play an A minor ninth chord, you would play this A minor note with the relative major seventh chord, which is a Cmaj7.

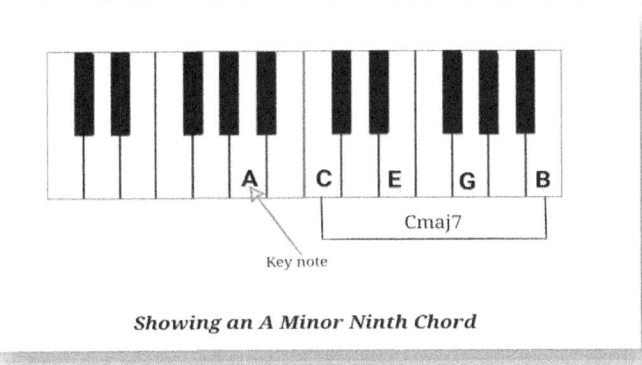

Showing an A Minor Ninth Chord

In playing this minor ninth chords, I prefer taking the ninth tone an octave lower, such that it is embedded in the minor ninth chord.

We've looked at how to form a C minor ninth and an A minor ninth chord. To form any minor ninth chord on the piano, you'd take a key, look for its relative major key, and play the major seventh chord of this relative major key. Adding the keynote and the seventh chord of the relative major key of this keynote, gives you a minor ninth chord.

Dominant Ninth Chords

Like major and minor ninth chords, dominant ninth chords are formed by simply adding the **ninth tone** to a **dominant seventh chord**. You can also see this chord as the keynote and an added III half diminished seventh chord (or IIImin7b5). In the key of C major, the III tone is an E tone, so by playing an E half diminished seventh chord (or Emin7b5) with the C note as bass, you've successfully formed the C dominant ninth chord (C9).

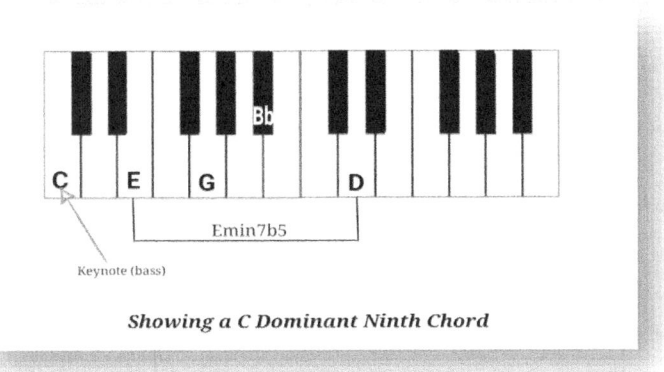

Showing a C Dominant Ninth Chord

Again, in playing this dominant ninth chords, I prefer taking the ninth tone an octave lower, in such a way that it is embedded in the chord.

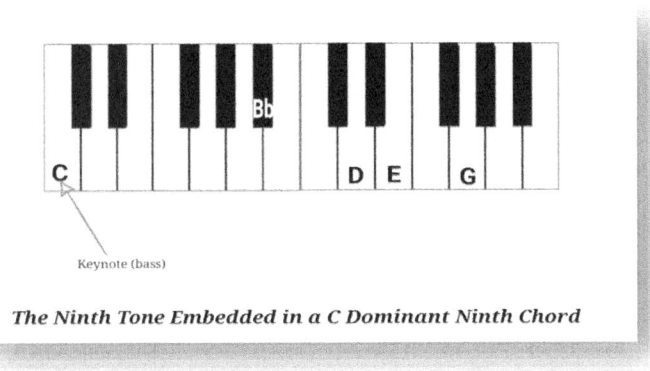

The Ninth Tone Embedded in a C Dominant Ninth Chord

To form the dominant ninth chord for any of the 12 keys on the piano, you'd first select a key, of which the dominant ninth chord you choose to form. From that selected major key, you'd form a half diminished seventh chord on the III tone. Playing the keynote as bass and the half diminished seventh chord formed on the III tone, gives you a dominant ninth chord.

Dominant Ninth Chords with an Added Sixth Note

This is simply adding a sixth tone to a dominant ninth chord. In the key of C major, this would be adding the A note to the C dominant ninth chord, giving you a C dominant ninth chord with an added sixth note (C9/6).

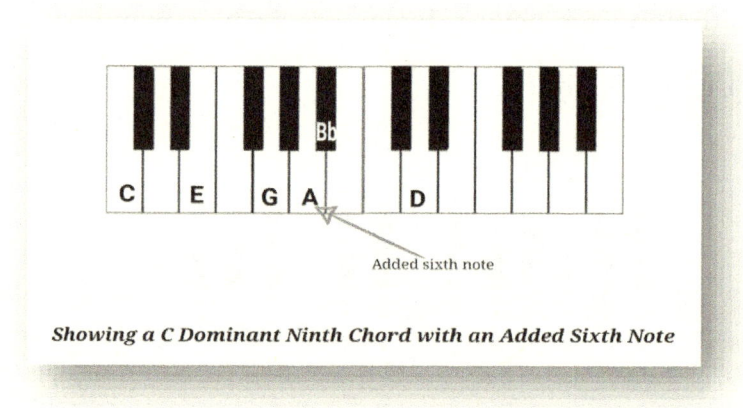

Showing a C Dominant Ninth Chord with an Added Sixth Note

Elvine Robert

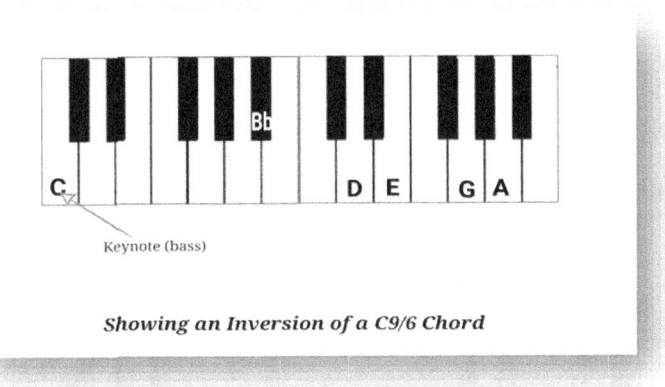

Showing an Inversion of a C9/6 Chord

Learning to Play the Min9 and Dom9/6 Chord

We'll be learning the minor ninth and dominant ninth chords; with an added sixth note, using the circle of fifth chart. This we will be doing by switching from a min9 chord to a dom9/6 chord.

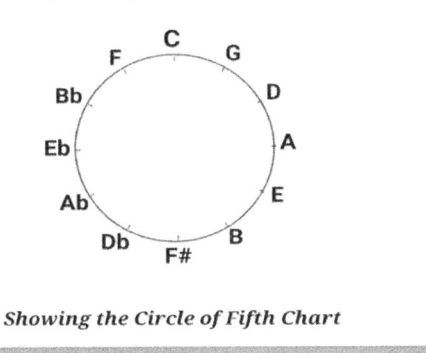

Showing the Circle of Fifth Chart

Starting from key C, by playing the Cmin9 and switching to an F9/6 chord, you've successfully gotten the pattern in which you would follow until you return back to the Cmin9 chord (i.e. alternating between min9 and Dom9/6 chords).

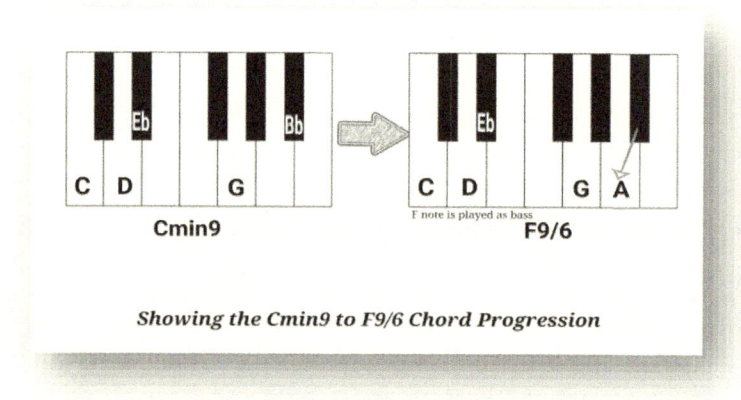

Showing the Cmin9 to F9/6 Chord Progression

From the above image, you'd play the Cmin9-F9/6-Bbmin9-Eb9/6-Abmin9-Db9/6…and so on, until the circle is complete. You would also notice that the min9 chords will include only half of the min9 chords since the other half are dom9/6 chords. To get the remaining half of the min9 and dom9/6 chords, you would start from the key of F, and so, you play the Fmin9-Bb9/6-Ebmin9-Ab9/6-Dbmin9-F#9/6…and so on, until the circle is complete.

Elvine Robert

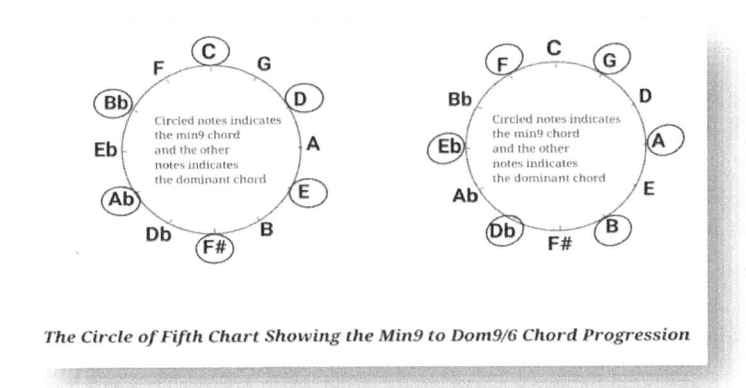

The Circle of Fifth Chart Showing the Min9 to Dom9/6 Chord Progression

In the image above, all you need to know is the min9 chords, because to get the next dominant chords, all you have to do is to lower the seventh tone of this min9 chord to form a dom9/6 chord. In playing these chords, you'd only need four fingers of your right hand, while you play the keynote as the bass note.

In playing these min9 and dom9/6 chords, it is much easier to use the 3rd inversion of the min9 chords because the seventh tone becomes the lowest tone of the chord and since we're reducing this seventh tone by a semitone, it is much easier to reduce the seventh note when at the bottom of a chord than when it is embedded in the middle of the chord.

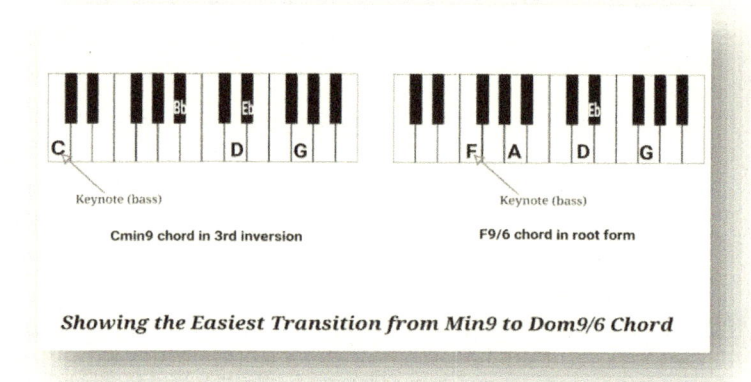

Beginner's Guide to Playing the Piano Professionally

Keynote (bass) — Cmin9 chord in 3rd inversion

Keynote (bass) — F9/6 chord in root form

Showing the Easiest Transition from Min9 to Dom9/6 Chord

By simply lowering this seventh tone, the next dom9/6 chord is formed.

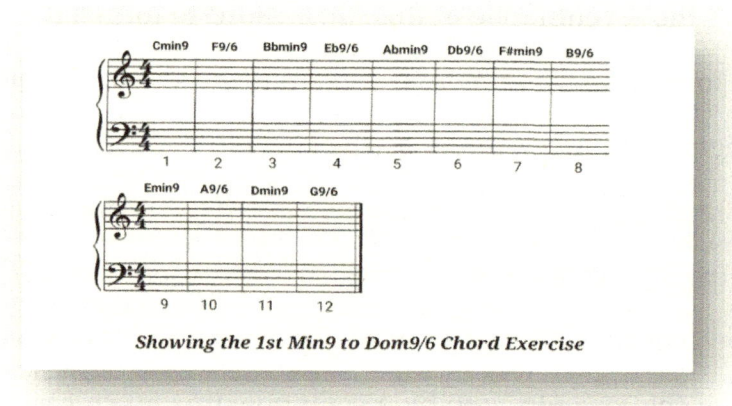

	Cmin9	F9/6	Bbmin9	Eb9/6	Abmin9	Db9/6	F#min9	B9/6
	1	2	3	4	5	6	7	8

	Emin9	A9/6	Dmin9	G9/6
	9	10	11	12

Showing the 1st Min9 to Dom9/6 Chord Exercise

Showing the 2nd Min9 to Dom9/6 Chord Exercise

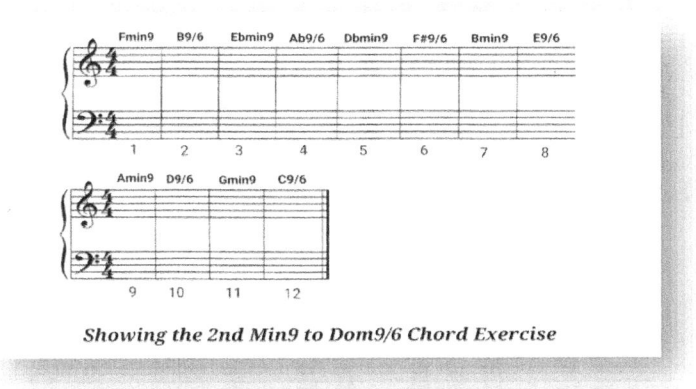

In the above images, all min9 chords and dom9/6 chords were covered. By practicing and getting more familiar with them, you'd be able to use these chords in playing a variety of songs.

The Min9 and Dom9/6 Chords to Resolve to the IV9

The I, IV and V chords are usually found to be dominant seventh, ninth or thirteenth chord in most gospel and blues song. In the previous chapters of this book, we looked at the I-IV chord progression or chord progressions having the I-IV chord progression as a part of them. Now, we'll be looking at how to add the II-V-I chords in-between this I-IV chord progression

The II-V-I chords to resolve to the IV chord

In reality, we are playing this II-V-I chords in the key of F major. This makes the C chord to be a dominant chord and the F chord the tonic for a moment.

Showing the II, V and I Tone in the Key of Fmaj

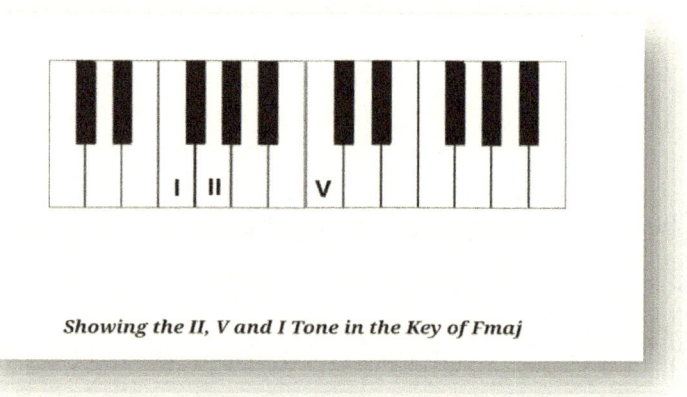

Imagine playing a song in the key of Cmaj and the chord progression is taking you, let's say from C to F (i.e. I-IV), instead of just moving from this C to F major chord, you would play a C9-Gmin9-C9/6-F9. This makes it sound like F is the tonic for a moment.

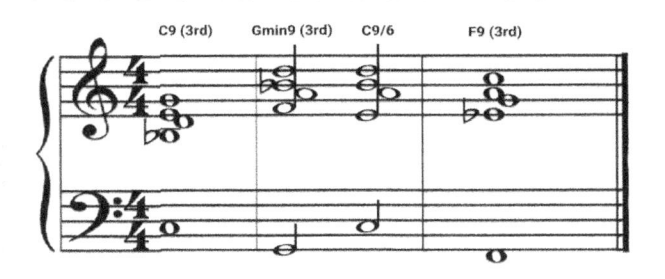

Showing the II-V-I Chord Progression Resolving to the IV Chord

In the above image, take note of the flats and also how the transition from Gmin9 (3rd) to C9/6 was achieved by just moving the seventh note a semitone lower. Also, note that in these ninth chords, the keynote was omitted and played as the bass note with the left hand.

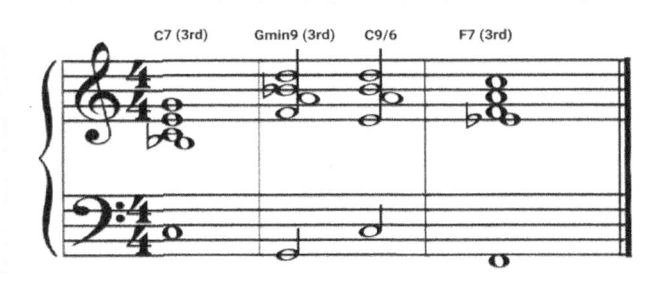

Using Seventh and Ninth Chords in the II-V-I to Resolve to the IV Chord

The III-VI-II-V-I to Resolve to the IV Chord

This is the same as the previous, but only that it is expanded by adding the III and VI chords. Do not forget that we are still in the key of C major.

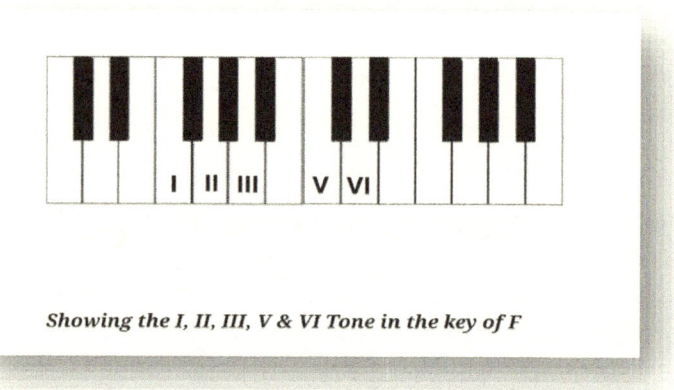

Showing the I, II, III, V & VI Tone in the key of F

This chord progression in the key of C major moves from C9-Amin9-D9/6-Gmin9-C9/6-F9. The chords start from Amin9 and moves to D9/6, then to Gmin9 before going to C9/6. Looking closely, you'd notice that these chords is like playing a II-V-I chord progression in the key of G and then another II-V-I in the key of F major.

Showing the III-VI-II-V-I Resolving to the IV Chord

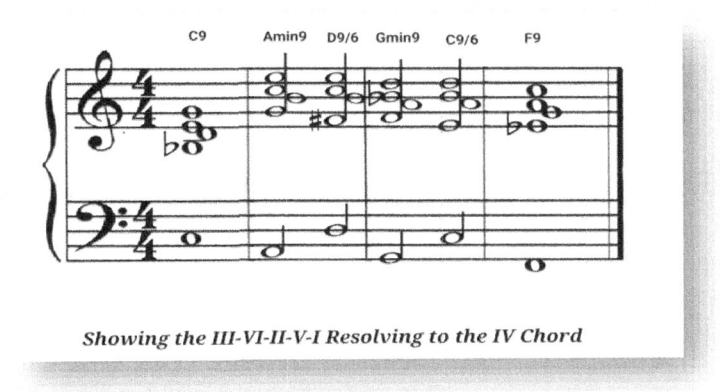

Try learning these chords in all twelve (12) keys and try to apply it in your piano play.

Note: In playing these chords to resolve to the IV chord, they are used as passing chords and nothing more.

Using the Ninth Chords to Replace the Seventh Chords

In the previous chapters, we looked at how to play the II-V-I chord progression using the seventh chords. Now, we'll be replacing this seventh chords with ninth chords.

The II-V-I chord progression using seventh chords in C major is Dmin7-G7-Cmaj7. By replacing this same chords with ninth chords, we have Dmin9-G9-Cmaj9.

Beginner's Guide to Playing the Piano Professionally

Replacing Seventh Chords with Ninth Chords

(II-V-I chord progression using seventh chords / II-V-I chord progression using ninth chords)

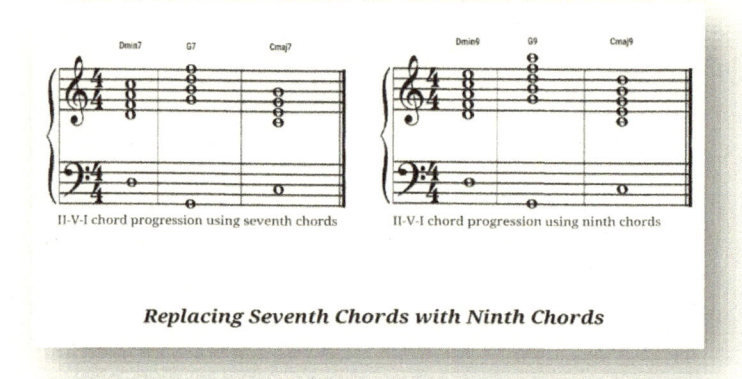

You'd notice that these ninth chords sound much fuller and sweeter to play.

The I-IV Turn-around with Ninth Chords

This chord progression is often called walking the bass and it is seen in most blues and gospel songs. This chord progression is usually used at the end of fast tempo Gospel music (i.e. praise songs).

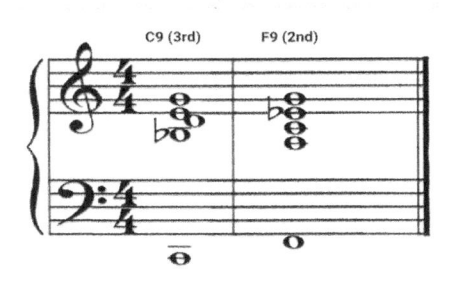

Showing the I9-IV9 Chord Progression in C Major

It is called walking the bass because the bass moves in a chromatic scale order, starting from the II tone. So, after playing the C9 chord, the bass moves from C to D before moving in a chromatic scale order to the F note.

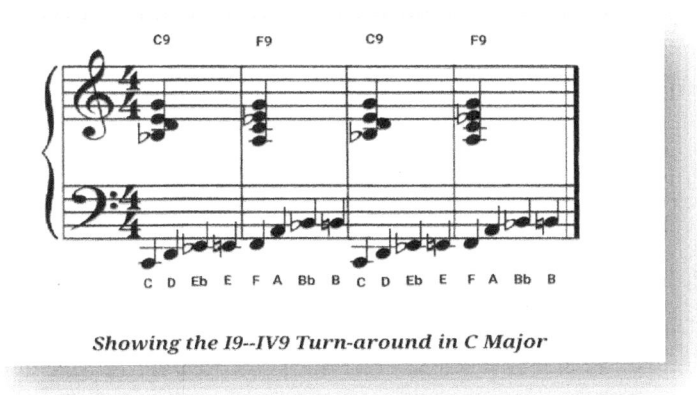

Showing the I9--IV9 Turn-around in C Major

Note: Chromatic scale is a scale that moves in semitones, such that it uses all the keys on the piano.

Chapter Summary

In this chapter, we looked at the ninth chords; which covers both the major, minor and dominant ninth chords. The major, minor and dominant ninth chords were formed by adding the ninth (9th) tone to a major, minor and dominant seventh chord. We also looked at how to use these ninth chords in chord progressions.

Chapter Seven

THE ELVENTH AND THIRTEENTH CHORDS

In the previous chapters, we looked at the three, four, and five toned chords (i.e. the triad, seventh and ninth chords respectively). In this chapter, we'll be looking at six and seven toned chords (i.e. the eleventh and thirteenth chords).

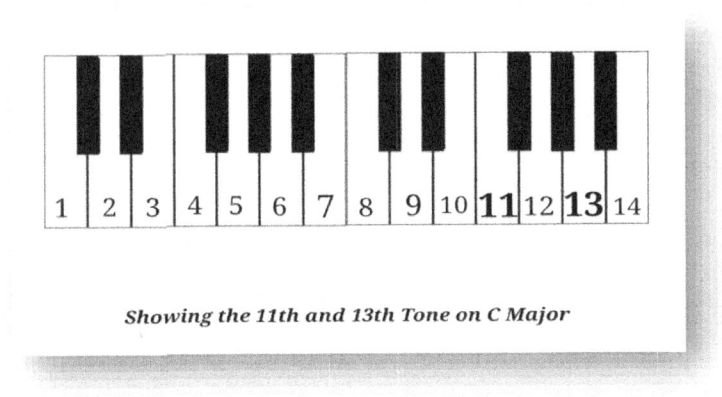

Showing the 11th and 13th Tone on C Major

Major Eleventh and Thirteenth Chords

These are chords which extends beyond the octave of a major scale. In forming the major eleventh chords, you'd simply add an **11th tone** to a **major ninth chord**. In the key of C major, this eleventh tone is an F note.

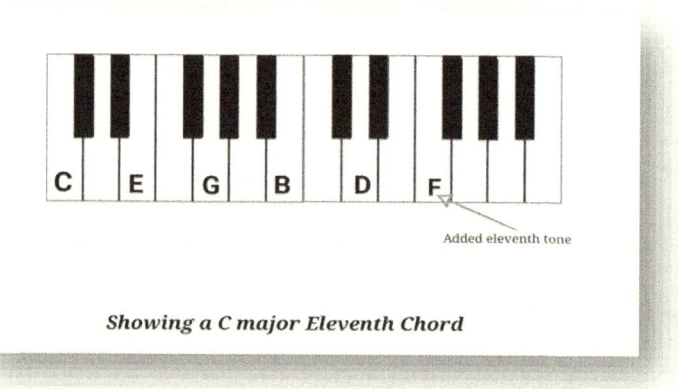

Showing a C major Eleventh Chord

In forming the major thirteenth chords, you'd simply add a **thirteenth tone** to a **major eleventh chord**. In the key of C major, this would be an A note.

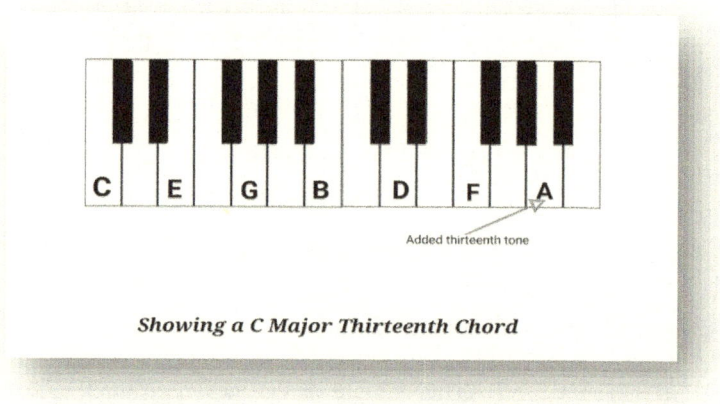

Showing a C Major Thirteenth Chord

In order to play these major 11th and 13th chords, you'd have to make use of both hands. You could also decide to experiment with different sounds by omitting some of these notes in the major eleventh and thirteenth chords. In omitting notes in chords, always remember that a major ninth chord includes a major seventh interval (or note), a major eleventh includes both a seventh and a ninth interval, and a major thirteenth chord includes a seventh, ninth, and eleventh.

Minor Eleventh and Thirteenth Chords

Just like the major eleventh and thirteenth chords, a minor eleventh chord is simply a minor ninth chord with an added eleventh tone. You could also see the minor eleventh chord as the addition of a I minor triad and VIIb major triad. This would be a Cmin and a Bbmaj triad in the key of C major (Cmin11=Cmin triad + Bbmaj triad).

Beginner's Guide to Playing the Piano Professionally

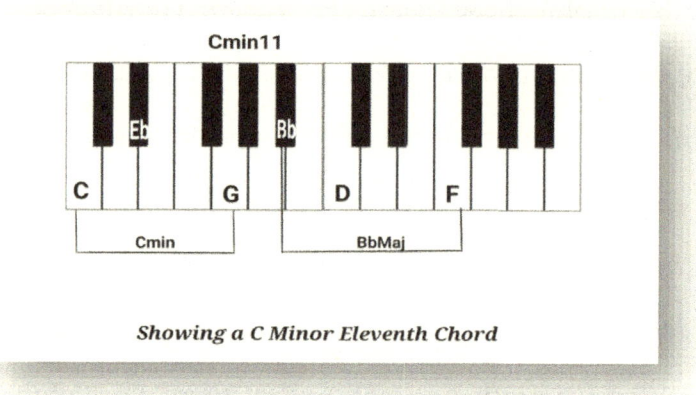

Cmin11

Cmin — BbMaj

Showing a C Minor Eleventh Chord

In forming the minor 13th chord, you would simply add a thirteenth tone to a minor eleventh chord. You could also see a minor thirteenth chord as an added I minor7 and a II minor triad (Imin7 + IImin triad). In the key of C major, this would be the addition of a Cmin7 and a Dmin triad (Cmin7 + Dmin triad).

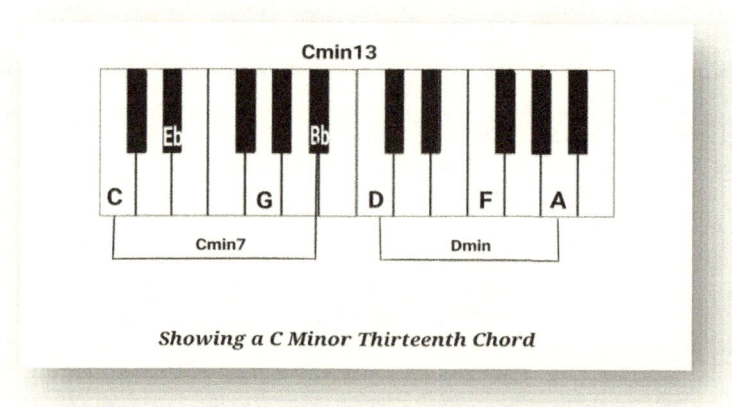

Cmin13

Cmin7 — Dmin

Showing a C Minor Thirteenth Chord

Note: The eleventh (11th) and thirteenth (13th) chords are also known as POLYCHORDS because they involve playing two different chords simultaneously.

Dominant Eleventh and Thirteenth Chords

The dominant eleventh chord is gotten by adding an eleventh tone to a dominant ninth chord. You could also see this chord as the addition of I major and VIIb major (C11 = Cmaj + Bbmaj).

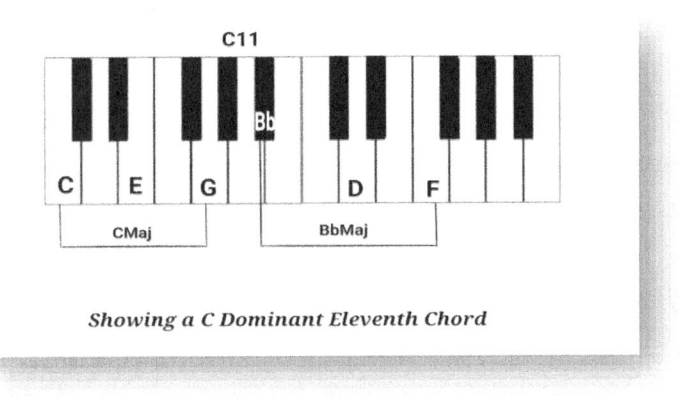

Showing a C Dominant Eleventh Chord

A dominant 13th chord is gotten by adding a thirteenth tone to a dominant eleventh chord. This chord can also be seen as the addition of I7 and a II minor (C13 = C7 + Dmin).

C13

Showing a C Dominant Thirteenth Chord

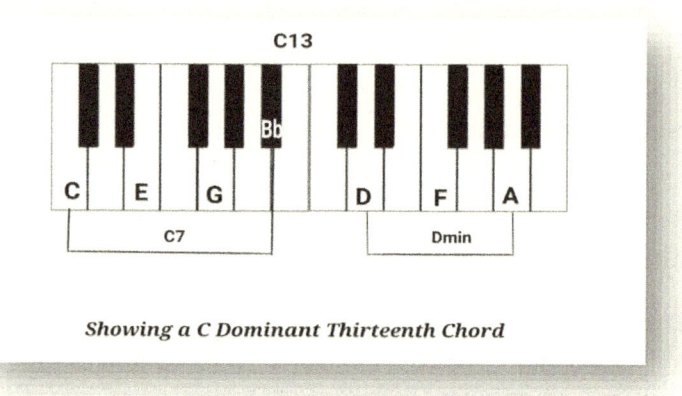

The dominant chords can be used to replace the seventh chords and because of its uniqueness, they could also be used for pretty much anything in the III-VI-II-V-I chord progression.

Learning to play the dominant thirteenth chords for the 12 keys on the piano would really improve your piano playing skill a great deal! This is because, the dominant thirteenth chords could be used as dominant preparations, secondary dominant as well as dominant and tonic chords.

Dominant Thirteenth Chords in the 12-bar Blues Progression

We've looked at the 12-bar blues progression with the seventh chords. In using the thirteenth chords, you simply need to replace this seventh dominant chords with the dominant thirteen chords.

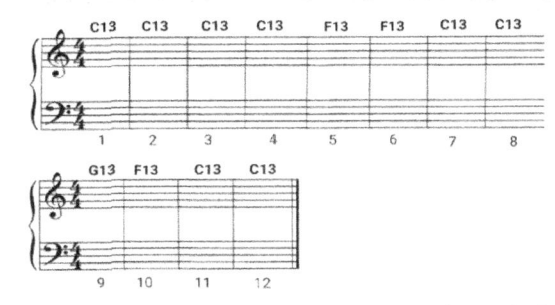

The 12-bar Blues Progression with Dominant Thirteenth Chords

Broken Chords

When notes are played together, it is called block chords, and when they are not played together, it is called broken chords.

When notes are played sequentially, one after the other, they are referred to as Arpeggio.

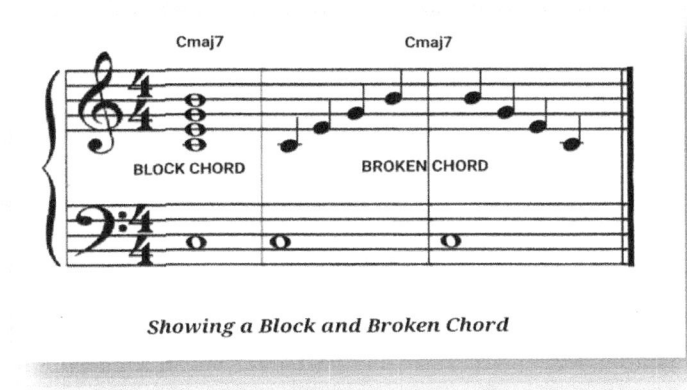

Showing a Block and Broken Chord

Beginner's Guide to Playing the Piano Professionally

You could use Arpeggios (or broken chords) in playing the piano to sound more interesting and fun.

Elvine Robert

Chapter Summary

This chapter was all about the eleventh and the thirteenth chords. We looked at how to form a major, minor and dominant eleventh and thirteenth chords by adding the eleventh and thirteenth tone to the right chords. These eleventh and thirteenth chords were referred to as POLYCHORDS because they involve playing two different chords at the same time.

In the level 3 of this series book, we'll be looking at alteration of chords, harmonizing of melodies, how to play various popular songs and lots more!

Made in the USA
Las Vegas, NV
02 April 2023